N

Cheesecake Love

Inventive, Irresistible, and
Super-Easy Cheesecake Desserts
for Every Day

JOCELYN BRUBAKER

THOMAS DUNNE BOOKS
ST. MARTIN'S GRIFFIN
NEW YORK

THOMAS DUNNE BOOKS.
An imprint of St. Martin's Press.

www.thomasdunnebooks.com
www.stmartins.com

Book design by Rita Sowins / Sowins Design

The Library of Congress Cataloging-in-Publication Data is available upon request.

ISBN 978-1-250-08446-0 (hardcover)
ISBN 978-1-250-08447-7 (e-book)

Our books may be purchased in bulk for promotional, educational, or business use.
Please contact your local bookseller or the Macmillan Corporate and Premium
Sales Department at 1-800-221-7945, extension 5442, or by e-mail at
MacmillanSpecialMarkets@macmillan.com.

First Edition: September 2017

10 9 8 7 6 5 4 3 2 1

To Jeremy, my best friend:
I love you more than
words can say.

To Cameron, Cassie,
and Caedon:
You are my inspiration
and joy!

Contents

·············· ✕ ··············

Introduction

WHY CHEESECAKE? WHY NOT!

My love for baking began at a young age. My first baking memory is from when I was four years old. I can remember my mom teaching me how to make a homemade piecrust from a recipe in one of my grandmother's old cookbooks. We rolled the crust out and filled it with cherries, and then I sat in front of the oven, watching it bake. That little pie gave me the baking bug that I have not been able to shake over the years. Back when I was younger, my mom would make almost everything from scratch with the help of my gram. I learned most of what I know about cooking and baking just from being in the kitchen, watching them and helping out.

Throughout my middle school and high school years, I spent many nights in the kitchen making treats to share with my youth group friends. Plus, by taking on the role of the baker/chief dinner maker in the family, I was able to get out of chores on our family farm! I would much rather work with a whisk than have to clean out horse stalls. One year, I was even brave enough to enter one of my cakes in the local county fair. I was so excited to get third place for my first-time entry.

While I was in college, I took a few cooking and baking classes that further deepened my love of being in the kitchen. After my husband and I got married, I worked outside the home for a year until we started having children. One of our desires was that I would be able to stay home and raise our kids while they were little. I continued to experiment in the kitchen with different dinners and desserts, and our kids helped me. Talk about learning patience quickly. Baking with small children makes you realize very quickly that flour will be everywhere and eggshells in your food are inevitable. But it also makes you cherish the moments teaching your children how to bake together.

One year I took a cake-decorating class at Michael's and started a small home-based cake-decorating business making birthday and wedding cakes for friends and family. After a few years of doing cakes, I realized that cake decorating was becoming a very tedious and stressful thing in my life. I am extremely particular when I bake, and it was taking me way too long to get the cakes decorated. Also, transporting wedding cakes in the back of your vehicle will test anyone's patience and sanity!

In 2008, I came across this thing called "blogging" and thought it could be a fun way to share photos of family life, crafts, and recipes with our family members who lived in other states. That first year, I only shared a handful of different things we did. It hadn't really caught on with me yet. The following year, our youngest son started school. After years of being a stay-at-home mom, I had no idea what to do with myself now that all three of our kids were in school. Since I definitely did not want to clean house or do laundry all day long, I began to search for a hobby that I could do during the day. I remembered that little blog I had started and thought it could be fun to start it back up again. After a few years of randomness, I realized that the posts that got the most comments and feedback were the fun and unique desserts I shared. I started to share a few more recipes each week, and then e-mails from people who were actually making my recipes started showing up in my inbox. Who knew my love of baking and being in the kitchen could generate so much interest?

From a Hobby to a Job

My husband had the opportunity to go into ministry full-time in 2012, and I realized blogging could potentially become a full-time job for me to help support our family. I was excited about the possibility of working at home, doing something I absolutely adored. Since then I have had the opportunity to travel to different places, work with brands, and meet people around the world who I would never have met if not for this fun job.

Over the years I have developed my own style when it comes to baking—I'm all about playful, approachable, inventive desserts that make you say "Wow!" Actually, my goal is to create recipes that make people say "Wow!" twice—first when they hear the name of the recipe (for instance, my Hot Chocolate Cheesecake Dip) and again when they realize how easy it is to make (only 15 minutes of prep before you can be dipping all the cookies and fruit in chocolate goodness). My kitchen style has definitely become a "semi-homemade with flair" approach. I always encourage others to give themselves a break and get some help from the store when they need it. Those box mixes were made for a reason, so do not feel bad about using them. I'm all for a delicious homemade cake every once in a while, but nine times out of ten, I make cake from a mix. It is easy to add a few extra things to a box mix to turn your creation into a dessert that everyone will go gaga for. To me, baking is about sharing the joy of delicious food with those we love, not about slaving in the kitchen for hours making everything from scratch.

Years of playing with my food in the kitchen has given me the confidence to make amazing semi-homemade desserts that make everyone take notice. It's your turn now.

Inspiration at the End of the Fork

Now that our children are in school all day, one of the things my husband and I enjoy doing is going on lunch or dinner dates regularly. Finding unique places with delicious food and decadent desserts is a hobby we have enjoyed doing together since we met. Over the years, we would always get a dessert or two to share at the end of our meal. And when I say share, I really mean he would eat a bite or two of his dessert, and I would finish off my piece and then eat the rest of his. The dessert we chose most often was a big slice of creamy cheesecake.

I can remember thinking that cheesecake was one of those desserts that was just too hard to manage in your own kitchen. I mean, who wants to deal with all the steps that go into making a fancy dessert, right?

Oh, how wrong I was! One day after eating out and enjoying a slice of $8 cheesecake, we started talking about how the cost of one slice at a restaurant probably cost the same as baking an entire cheesecake in our own kitchen. My husband started experimenting with different cheesecake recipes at first. Eventually the lure of creamy cheesecake got me to start experimenting with different crusts and crazy cheesecake combos, too. I was instantly hooked. It also did not take me much time to realize that cheesecake is really not that hard to make, if you follow some easy steps.

Cheesecake All the Things

Since those first days of cheesecake experiments, I have learned to work cheesecake into any and every dessert you can think of. Brownies, fudge, cookies, pie, and pastries have all become a blank canvas for some cheesecake love. If it doesn't have cheesecake in it, it should. How's that for a baking motto?

Cheesecake has become one of my absolute favorite thing to bake (and one of the most popular dessert types on the blog), so when I was approached about creating an entire book about cheesecake, I was instantly intrigued. How many more ways could I put cheesecake into desserts? I started making a list of flavors and combos as we worked on the book proposal. After developing all the recipes in this book, I have not even gotten through half that list yet. I definitely see way more cheesecake in my life!

Over the years, I have learned that cheesecake does not need to be hard or boring, or even traditional. It should be fun—it's the perfect canvas for any flavor, and it can be easily adapted to be a bar, a pie, a cookie filling, a cupcake, even a parfait or a cake layer. It is my hope and desire that these recipes will inspire others to create their own unique desserts and, ultimately, to find the same excitement and creativity in the kitchen that I found so many years ago! So set out some cream cheese, and get ready to cheesecake all the things

Baking Equipment

Over my years spent working in different kitchens, I have developed a love for baking pans and kitchen gadgets. You know, those fun little utensils and tools that are designed to make life in the kitchen a little easier. My husband and I enjoy going into local kitchen stores and eyeballing the fun gadgets they sell. Now most people do not have the storage to be able to buy all the things that you could use in your kitchen. And to be honest, a lot of these kitchen toys are not really necessary. It's easy to get caught up in the moment when you are in the store looking at fun gadgets, but most of the time, those kitchen tools get used once and go in a drawer, never to be seen again. Don't waste your money on tools you really do not need—save that money for more cream cheese and chocolate chips.

These are the pans and kitchen tools that I like to use regularly in our kitchen. This list of kitchen equipment will help you if you plan on baking treats more often for your family and friends.

Baking Pans

Without them, your oven would be a complete mess!

> SPRINGFORM PANS <

Do not be intimidated by the name. A springform pan is just a fancy word for a cake pan with a removable bottom. The two pieces of this pan are a flat metal bottom and a metal ring that wraps around the bottom. The metal sides buckle onto the bottom of the pan, creating a tight seal that keeps the batter from leaking out of the pan as it bakes.

Items made in springform pans are also cooled in the pan. After cooling, the ring is unlatched and the sides are lifted off, which makes it easy to remove the cake in perfect condition for serving. Most cake pans have to be flipped upside down to remove the cake from inside of them. This is not a good idea when you are making a delicate item like a cheesecake or a coffee cake with streusel. That would turn your amazing creation into a horrendous mess. With a springform pan, you simply detach the sides, keeping your cake beautiful.

To make the cheesecakes in this book, you will need a set of 8-, 9-, and 10-inch round springform pans that are 3 inches tall.

> BAKING SHEETS <

A baking sheet is just a metal tray. There are two basic types of baking sheets: those with sides (rimmed), and those without sides. Baking sheets without sides are often used for cookies, as they let the heat from the oven flow freely around the cookies, allowing them to bake evenly. I have a set of baking sheets without sides that I use for almost every cookie I make.

The color of the baking sheet can affect the outcome of your cookies, too. Dark pans absorb more heat energy, causing cookies to be overdone or darker on the bottom. I prefer light-colored pans, so my cookies do not overbake or get too dark while baking. Look for heavy-duty pans that will hold up to many years of baking.

Other types of baking sheets have sides. They are more of a general-purpose pan. You will need a 12 x 18-inch rimmed baking sheet to create a steam bath under your cheesecakes. I do not recommend using a baking sheet much larger than this because it will block the heat and airflow in the oven, causing baked goods to bake unevenly. We will talk about the practice and purpose of the steam bath later in the book. And no, this type of steam bath is not a spa treatment, despite the name!

> JELLY ROLL PAN <

A jelly roll pan is a 10 x 15-inch version of a rimmed baking sheet. The sides in a jelly roll pan are about 1 inch high, making it good for making sponge cakes and cake rolls. Jelly roll pans should be made of sturdy metal to keep the pan from warping in a hot oven and making the cake batter spill to one side. I recently tried to cook a cake roll on a thin metal pan. The heat caused the pan to warp, and I had crispy cake on one side and raw cake on the other. No one wants this kind of uneven cake roll in his or her life. Ain't nobody got time for that!

> CAKE PANS <

Cake pans are metal pans that come in a variety of shapes and sizes and are used for baking cakes or brownies. I recommend having two each of the following sizes: 9 x 13-inch rectangular, 8-inch square, 8-inch round, and 10-inch round. Pay attention to the height of the pan called for in the recipe. Some cake pans have 1-inch sides, while others have 2- or 3-inch sides. If you try to put too much batter into a cake pan with shorter sides, it will overflow into the bottom of your oven as it bakes. This is not a mess you want to deal with, trust me!

Make sure to grease and flour your pans thoroughly before adding your batter. This will ensure that your cake or brownie comes out of the pan in one piece. I like to use nonstick baking sprays with and without flour added to them. You can also grease and flour your pans by hand if you prefer that method.

For bar cookies and brownies, I recommend lining the pan with aluminum foil before spraying it with nonstick baking spray. (Make sure you read the tips and tricks section for a fun way to line your pan with foil.) Leave a slight overhang of foil, and then when the baked good has cooled, you can lift it out of the pan easily using the foil as handles. This allows you to cut the item into nicer squares, as well as cutting down on your kitchen cleanup time. Work smarter, not harder!

> CUPCAKE PANS <

A cupcake pan (or muffin tin) is a pan with multiple cups, allowing you to make small individual-size desserts. I recommend two standard nonstick pans with 12 cups each. Most cake mixes and batters make about 24 servings, so having two pans allows you to bake all of them at once. If you have leftover batter and need to bake just a few more cupcakes, fill the empty cups with water to help the remaining cupcakes bake evenly.

> MINI-CUPCAKE PANS <

These are the same as a cupcake pan (or muffin tin), but in a smaller form. Most of these pans come with 24 cups. You definitely want two of these pans for making mini treats. Most mini dessert recipes make a lot, so you want to bake as many at a time as you can.

> PIE PLATES <

Pie plates have shallow, sloping sides with a rim to hold the crust in place. These plates are one piece, unlike springform pans, and can be made of aluminum, metal, or glass. A standard pie plate is 9 inches wide and 1¼ inches deep, although they do come in 9½ inches and 10 inches and deep-dish versions as well. A deep-dish pie plate will be 1½ to 2 inches deep, allowing for more filling to be baked. It is very important to read your recipe beforehand to see what size is recommended. Too much batter in a shallow pan is a recipe for disaster! I have a standard 9-inch pie plate and a 10-inch deep-dish pie plate that I used for all the pie recipes in this book.

> TART PANS <

A tart pan is similar to a pie plate. The tart pan has straight sides that may be fluted. These pans are generally made of metal with a removable bottom that allows you to get the dessert out without damaging the sides of the crust. It is similar to a springform pan but it does not "lock" together or form a tight seal. This works well for desserts with crusts. The crust keeps the liquid from coming out of the bottom of the pan. I do not recommend putting a liquid into an unlined tart pan. Tart pans come in a variety of sizes and shapes.

For most recipes, I recommend one 9-inch tart and one mini-tart pan with 12 cavities. The mini-tart pan looks very similar to the standard pan, but it does not have a removable bottom. You can also use a mini-tart pan for making little pies (like Mini Orange Cream Cheesecake Pies, page 175).

Kitchen Utensils & Tools

Oh yeah! More gadgets to play with!

> SILICONE SPATULAS <

A spatula is a kitchen tool that has a handle and a silicone blade. These are used for scraping the sides of bowls, mixing ingredients, and spreading frosting. Spatulas come in many sizes and varieties. I highly recommend having a few in each size because you will use them multiple times in a recipe.

I like using larger rubber spatulas for scraping dough and batter off the sides of my mixing bowls as the ingredients are coming together. They are also good to use when you are cooking in nonstick pans, as metal can scratch or otherwise damage a nonstick surface. A smaller rubber spatula is also great for filling measuring cups with peanut butter or sour cream.

> METAL SPATULAS <

These tools usually have a metal blade and a wooden handle to insulate them from the heat. Again, these come in a variety of sizes and shapes. I recommend a larger one with an offset blade (where the blade is angled to sit lower than the handle) for removing cookies from baking sheets.

> FROSTING SPATULA <

A frosting spatula is very similar to a metal spatula. They are made of the same ingredients. The main difference is in the blade. A frosting spatula has a much smaller surface. This allows you to spread frosting evenly on a flat surface.

I highly recommend a small offset frosting spatula. This is a spatula that has the blade lower than the handle. It makes it much easier to frost the tops of cakes and to spread batter in pans.

> ROLLING PIN <

A rolling pin is a kitchen tool that allows you to flatten and shape dough. They are generally cylinder shaped with small handles on either end. You can also use a rolling pin to crush cookies and crackers in plastic bags when you are making a crust for your cheesecake.

> WHISK <

This utensil has a narrow handle and wire or plastic loops joined together on the end. Whisks are used for mixing ingredients smoothly or for incorporating air into a mixture quickly.

I recommend having a whisk attachment for your mixer for making some toppings (like homemade Whipped Cream, page 29). A handheld whisk is good to have in your kitchen for making toppings that don't require a long whisk time (like Lemon Curd, page 27, or Caramel Topping, page 25).

> STAND MIXER <

A stand mixer has a frame that houses the motor. It also has a mounting base to hold the bowl in place as it works. They come in a variety of colors to match your kitchen décor, if desired.

I grew up using a hand mixer for everything I made. Trust me, making multiple batches of frosting and cookie dough takes a lot longer that way. My husband surprised me with a Kitchen Aid stand mixer for my birthday one year, and I have never gone back to that hand mixer again. A stand mixer is more expensive, but it is totally worth every penny, in my book. Mixing things like frosting and cookie dough is much easier when you have a mixer that can handle it. Plus, if you are a multitasker like me, you can turn on the mixer and then work on another aspect of the recipe (and yes, we are getting to those soon!). If all you have is a hand mixer, do not despair. You can make every recipe in this book with that handheld tool as well. Just add that stand mixer to your birthday or Christmas list ASAP!

> FOOD PROCESSOR <

This electric appliance is used to chop, slice, dice, crush, or mix ingredients easily. Make sure you purchase one that is big enough to accommodate how you want to use it. I love using mine to crush cookies and crackers for crusts, but I also use it for making homemade pie dough (see Piecrust, page 22).

> PIPING BAGS AND TIPS <

Piping bags are triangular bags made of plastic or cloth. You use them to squeeze and press soft ingredients through the narrow end that is fitted with a metal or plastic icing tip.

Icing tips come in many shapes and sizes and are used for decorating baked goods. The tips I use most often for cakes and cheesecakes are the Wilton tips 21 (open star), 27 (closed star), 2D (drop flower), and 1M (swirl). You can find these tips in the baking aisle at most craft stores. I love using them to pipe whipped cream, Cool Whip, or frosting on top of cakes and cheesecakes. The icing tips make these toppings look a little more professional with very little effort. Most of those craft stores also offer classes on how to decorate cakes like a pro.

Basic Baking Tips

MAKING LIFE EASIER

> READ THE RECIPE <

Make sure you take the time to read the entire recipe you are making, fully and completely, before you start baking. You want to make sure you understand each step and what is required to get that sweet treat at the end. Also, make sure you have enough time set aside to completely finish a recipe. Most kitchen-baking fails happen because you end up rushing through steps because you do not have enough time. Not like that has ever happened to me…okay, maybe more than once!

> PAY ATTENTION <

Pay attention to details in the recipe instructions like creaming, folding, or mixing. These are all different ways of mixing in certain ingredients. I know it would be easier to just dump it all in the bowl and let it mix, but there are reasons for each step being separated. Baking is a science. Follow the order of the recipe, and make sure you do each step completely and thoroughly before moving on to the next one. Any changes that you make to the recipe could affect the outcome of your baked goods.

> PULL OUT YOUR INGREDIENTS <

Set out all the ingredients on your counter before you get started. This way you can see if you are missing an ingredient. There is nothing more frustrating than getting halfway through a recipe and realizing you are out of sugar or flour just when you need it.

> IS IT EXPIRED? <

Check the expiration dates on things like flour, baking powder, and baking soda regularly. Expired ingredients will not work properly in a recipe, causing your dessert to be flat and dense.

> TO CREAM OR NOT TO CREAM <

Cream cheese and butter need to be set out at least 30 minutes before you use them in a recipe. This allows these ingredients to come to room temperature naturally. When cream cheese and butter are softer, it is easier to beat them into a creamy mixture.

If you do forget to set the cream cheese out ahead of time, you can unwrap it and very carefully microwave it until soft. I will usually do this in 5-second increments, flipping it over each time, until it is slightly soft.

Make sure to beat the cream cheese first before adding any other ingredients. This helps to get it nice and creamy. Adding sugar to the mixture next will help smooth out any extra lumps that may still be in the cream cheese. I like to beat the mixture until the cream cheese and sugar are a very smooth mixture! Starting with a smooth, creamy mixture makes it much easier to mix in the rest of the cheesecake ingredients.

Do not be afraid to use your spatula many times in the creaming process. This essential kitchen tool is great for scraping the bowls and moving the ingredients down into the bottom of the bowl where the blades can mix it together better. It is a good idea to have extra spatulas to measure and scrape different ingredients.

> REAL BUTTER IS BEST <

Use real butter when a recipe calls for it. Butter and margarine are two different products and work in two different ways. Butter is a natural product made from cream and is better for baking because of its high fat content. This fat contributes to tenderness and flakiness in your baked goods. Margarine is not a natural product. It is made by adding hydrogen to oil and is composed of mostly water. That extra water in margarine can affect your cookies and cakes.

When baking, I always use unsalted butter because this allows me to control the amount of salt in a recipe. If all you have on hand is salted butter, just adjust the amount of salt you add later.

Cut your butter into small pieces to help it soften faster. Do not microwave your butter to soften it. Even a few seconds can melt the butter, which can affect how your cookies or cakes bake. If a recipe calls for melted butter, you can use a microwave to do that. Just make sure you only do 10-second increments; otherwise, your microwave will be coated in butter from top to bottom. Take my word on that one.

> CHOOSING AN EGG <

The size of egg you use makes a difference in recipes. Eggs add moisture to your batter, so using a different-size egg than is called for will throw off the ratio of dry and wet ingredients. This could result in your baked goods being too dry or too wet in the end. I used large eggs for every recipe in this book.

> PREHEAT YOUR OVEN <

Remember to preheat your oven before you begin a recipe. All ovens are different and heat up at different rates. Putting a pan of batter into an oven that is not at the right temperature will cause it to bake slower and unevenly. Using an oven thermometer is a great way to see if your oven is actually baking at the temperature at which you set.

Once you place the product into the oven, do not open the oven door to check on it until it has baked for at least three-quarters of the baking time. You want to maintain a consistent oven temperature for as long as possible.

Equally important is the use of a timer. Make sure you set a timer to remind you to take the food out of the oven. Also, make sure you are in hearing range of this timer. It's always a sad day for dessert when your cakes, cookies, or cheesecake are dry and over baked.

> USING FOIL AND PARCHMENT PAPER <

I like to line all my pans with parchment paper or aluminum foil. Not only does this keep the food from sticking to the pan, but it also makes getting a dessert out of your baking pan so much easier. Leave an extra bit of paper or foil at the top so you can lift your cake or brownies right out. Not to mention that cleanup time in the kitchen is a whole lot easier when all you have to do is throw away the liners.

Here is a quick tip on lining a pan with foil that completely amazed my husband the first time he saw me doing it. First, turn your pan upside down and place it on the counter. Second, form the foil to the outside of the pan creating a foil mold. Third, remove the foil and turn the pan right-side up. Finally, place the foil mold inside the pan and press it into place. This should be a pretty good fit. And it makes everyone think you are awesome when they watch you do it! Thank you, Pinterest, for keeping me cool!

Make sure you hold your pan over the sink when you coat the foil with baking spray. This way all the excess spray goes into the sink instead of all over your counters and floors.

> HOW TO SCOOP FLOUR <

Make sure you measure your flour properly. If you scoop flour out of your container with the measuring cup, it will pack it down, which in turn adds more flour to your recipe. Extra flour in a recipe can create a heavy, dried-out baked good, which is never a good idea.

Use a spoon to stir your flour up a bit, and then spoon the flour gently into the measuring cup, mounding it over the top. Use a flat object like a butter knife or spatula to scrape the excess flour back into the container. Never shake the excess flour off the top of the measuring cup, as this will pack the flour down, too.

> DO NOT OVERMIX <

Be very careful not to overmix your cheesecake batter after adding liquids like heavy cream and eggs. Beating these liquids too much and too quickly produces air bubbles in the batter. As those air bubbles bake, they push the batter out, creating pockets. This is one reason that a cheesecake may crack as it bakes.

> WATER BATH VERSUS STEAM BATH <

There is great debate over whether to bake a cheesecake in a water bath or to steam it. Both ways will increase the moisture in your oven, and as the cheesecake bakes, that extra moisture keeps your end product nice and creamy.

To bake a cheesecake in a water bath, you cover the bottom of the cheesecake pan with foil and then place it directly into a roasting pan of hot water in the oven. To steam a cheesecake, you simply bake the cheesecake on the oven rack above a pan of water.

Either way will work, but I like that steam baths are less work, and there is no chance of water leaking into my delicious cheesecake (as there is with a water bath). I like to place a large rimmed baking sheet on the very bottom rack of my oven and fill it halfway with water. As the oven preheats, the water starts to heat up and create steam. Always place your cheesecake on the oven rack right above the water. There is no need to wrap your pan or place the cheesecake into the water using this method.

One word of warning: When you open the oven door to either put the pan in or remove the pan, give the steam a second to escape before reaching in with your hands or face. Otherwise, be prepared to get a steamy, hot facial.

> IS IT DONE? <

Cheesecake often looks underbaked when you take it out of the oven. A good rule of thumb is to wiggle the pan gently. If the entire cheesecake moves, it is not done baking yet. If just 2 to 3 inches of the center jiggles a little, it is done. The center will also appear to be moist, but should never be runny.

Cheesecake has to cool and set up before it is actually finished, so give it time to chill. The center will get firmer the longer it chills. Make sure you do not overbake your cheesecakes. Another main reason a cheesecake cracks is because it was baked too long. If you see a lot of browning along the edges or big cracks, you overbaked it. Keep in mind that some small cracking along the edges is okay, because as the cheesecake cools, the cracks will settle back into the top.

Take the cheesecake out of the oven as soon as it is done. There is no need to keep it in the oven for extra time. I know everyone has differing opinions on this, but every cheesecake in this book was taken out and placed on a wire rack immediately after the timer went off. I'm a rebel like that! Leaving a cheesecake in the hot/warm oven will cause it to continue to bake, which in turn increases the risk for cracks and a dried-out cheesecake. That would be no bueno!

Cool the cheesecake for 5 minutes on the wire rack, then immediately run a sharp knife around the top edge of the cheesecake between the cheesecake and the pan. This is very important, because it loosens the cheesecake from the springform pan. As the cheesecake cools, it will start to shrink slightly. If the cheesecake is still attached to the sides of the pan, it will pull apart the soft center in the middle, creating a crack.

Realize that even if you follow every step in this book, cracks are bound to happen. Be prepared to see cracks in a cheesecake at some point in your baking career. Even the pros have off days and get cracks. Melted chocolate, whipped cream, and/or fruit will be your best friend when that happens. Just cover that crack up with some goodness, and no one will ever know about it. They will be too busy stuffing their face with your creamy cheesecake to look for imperfections.

> MAKING PERFECT CUTS <

Use a hot, sharp knife to make perfect cuts in your baked goods for serving. I usually run a knife under very hot water and then dry it off in between each cut I make in a dessert. You can also use this hot, dry knife to smooth the sides of the dessert as well. This process takes a little longer (and you will probably have to keep everyone who is dying to eat it back) but the results make for a pretty presentation…then devour it!

And last, but most important, have fun while you are baking. Be open to your own creativity. Every baker is different and has different ideas about what flavors work together. How boring would life be if we all liked the same things? Play with different crust ideas or mix-ins after you get comfortable baking a recipe. Most of the recipes in this book can be used interchangeably. Don't like a certain fruit or candy mix-in or cookie that I used? Prefer a Butterfinger Cheesecake Pie over the Snickers Cheesecake Pie on page 163? Go ahead and change out the candy bar for one that you love. Tweak the recipe, and do you! Baking is all about trial and error. Yes, it may fail, but you will learn from those mistakes, and that just means more time in the kitchen perfecting your baking.

Stocking the Cheesecake Love Pantry

One of the best ways to make baking manageable on busy weeknights is to stock your pantry with all the components you might need—everything from mixes to fillings to toppings. Sometimes you'll want to go for a store-bought shortcut. I'm all about using a boxed cake mix or brownie mix and jazzing them up to look homemade. But I have found that it is also just as easy to make these mixes in your own kitchen. Think homemade apple pie filling and caramel topping are too hard to make? Think again. I'll show you just how easy it is to create your own toppings, fillings, and brownie mixes in no time!

Single-Batch Homemade Brownies

PREP TIME: 20 MINUTES | **BAKE TIME:** 25 TO 30 MINUTES | **SERVING:** MAKES 12 BROWNIES

Our youngest absolutely loves brownies, but they have to be plain brownies. Any time I add any extra things like chocolate chips or frosting, he gives me a sad-puppy-dog look of disappointment. So when I found a recipe for homemade brownies in an old church cookbook, I knew I had to give it a try. After a few tweaks and variations, I came up with a brownie that we all love. It is great by itself, but it also is great for making trifles, cheese-cake brownies, and cakes. I prefer to make these amazing brownies with a dark cocoa powder, as indicated in the recipe. This gives the brownie a richer flavor. Feel free to use regular cocoa powder if you prefer.

INGREDIENTS

½ cup (1 stick) unsalted butter

¼ cup unsweetened dark cocoa powder

2 large eggs

1 cup sugar

1 teaspoon vanilla extract

½ teaspoon salt

¾ cup all-purpose flour

¼ teaspoon baking powder

INSTRUCTIONS

1. Preheat the oven to 350°F. Line an 8-inch square baking pan with aluminum foil and coat the foil with nonstick baking spray.

2. Melt the butter in a small saucepan over low heat. Whisk in the cocoa powder until it has dissolved. Let the mixture cool slightly.

3. Beat the eggs in a medium bowl for 2 to 3 minutes. Add the sugar and vanilla and beat again.

4. Quickly whisk ¼ cup of the hot melted butter mixture into the egg mixture. This will warm the eggs up gradually, so they do not scramble. Add the rest of the butter mixture and beat until incorporated.

5. Sift together the salt, flour, and baking powder into a medium bowl. Slowly beat the dry ingredients into the wet ingredients. Do not overmix the batter.

6. Spread the batter in the prepared pan. Bake the brownies for 25 to 28 minutes, or until a toothpick inserted into the center comes out mostly clean.

7. Place the pan on a wire rack and let the brownies cool before cutting them into 12 squares.

VARIATION:

Double-Batch Homemade Brownies
- » Double the ingredients.
- » Spread the batter in a prepared 9 x 13-inch baking pan.
- » Bake at 350°F for 30 minutes.
- » Let cool and then cut into 24 squares.

Optional Ways to Jazz Up Your Brownies
- » Stir ½ cup mini chocolate chips or nuts into the batter right before spreading it in the pan.
- » Dust the finished brownies with powdered sugar.
- » Slather the finished brownies with a thick layer of frosting.
- » Drizzle the finished brownies with homemade caramel topping.

Piecrust

PREP TIME: 5 MINUTES | **SERVING:** MAKES 1 (9-INCH) PIECRUST

As a teenager, I always made my piecrusts from scratch when I was baking. After my husband and I got married, I started using store-bought crusts. They were just easier to use and took less time when I had little ones helping me in the kitchen. Recently, I decided I wanted to try to make those crusts from scratch again, so I came up with this easy recipe. I wanted the flakiness that shortening gives along with the flavor that butter adds, so I used both. I love that this crust can be made in a food processor with just a few pulses. Give it a try. You'll be surprised at how easy this is.

INGREDIENTS

1¼ cups all-purpose flour

½ teaspoon salt

4 tablespoons (½ stick) cold unsalted butter

¼ cup vegetable shortening

3 tablespoons ice water

INSTRUCTIONS

1. Place the flour, salt, butter, and shortening in a food processor. Pulse a few times until the mixture resembles large coarse crumbs.

2. Add in the water 1 tablespoon at a time, pulsing after each addition.

3. Gather the dough together and form a ball. Wrap the dough ball in plastic wrap and refrigerate for at least 1 hour.

4. Using a rolling pin, roll the dough out on a floured surface to a 9½-inch circle. Fold the dough in half and then in half again. Lift the dough gently and place it in a 9-inch pie plate that has been sprayed with nonstick spray. Unfold the dough to line the pan.

5. Fold the edges of the dough underneath and crimp the edges with your fingers. Bake according to the recipe directions.

Note. The dough ball can be wrapped and refrigerated for up 5 days. But really, why wait? Turn to the pie chapter and start making some cheesecake pie, stat!

Cookie Dough Bites

PREP TIME: 30 MINUTES | **SERVING:** MAKES 56 COOKIE DOUGH BITES

When we were kids, my brother and sisters and I would always fight over who got to lick the bowl and spatula whenever our mom made cookies. And my three kids do the same thing whenever I'm baking cookies or cakes now, too. These easy cookie bites are a way to enjoy that cookie dough without the threat of raw eggs. Add them to fudge or brownies or eat them plain—I won't judge.

INGREDIENTS

4 tablespoons (½ stick) unsalted butter, at room temperature

⅓ cup packed brown sugar

½ teaspoon vanilla extract

Pinch of salt

½ cup all-purpose flour

1 teaspoon milk

¼ cup mini chocolate chips

INSTRUCTIONS

1. Place the butter, brown sugar, vanilla, and salt in a bowl and beat until creamy.

2. Add the flour, vanilla, and milk and beat again until a soft dough forms.

3. Gently stir in the chocolate chips.

4. Roll the cookie mixture into 56 small balls, each roughly the size of a marble. These can be placed on a wax paper–lined tray and frozen for 30 minutes. Store in a plastic freezer bag for up to one month.

Caramel Dip or Topping

PREP TIME: 5 MINUTES PLUS COOL TIME | **COOK TIME:** 10 TO 12 MINUTES | **SERVING:** MAKES 1 CUP

I absolutely love eating caramel, whether it is salted, drizzled over brownies, stirred into cheesecake, or spooned over my ice cream. I'll take it any way I can get it. Until recently, making homemade caramel scared me. All that bubbling and having to get the color just right made me run. I would head to the store and buy a jar of caramel every time I needed caramel for a recipe. But I decided this was a fear that needed to be conquered. After trying out a few different things, I finally came up with a creamy caramel dip that tastes amazing. Forget dipping anything in this caramel because you will be eating it from the jar with a spoon. Here's to conquering fear!

INGREDIENTS

1 cup sugar

¼ cup water

2 tablespoons unsalted butter

⅔ cup heavy cream

1 to 2 teaspoons coarse sea salt (optional)

INSTRUCTIONS

1. Place the sugar and water in a 3-quart saucepan with high sides. Pick up the pan and rotate it around to get the water into all the sugar. Place the pan over medium heat and cook until the sugar has dissolved. Do not stir the mixture at all.

2. The mixture will begin to bubble. Let the sugar mixture cook for 8 to 10 minutes more. Again, do not stir the mixture at all while it is bubbling.

3. The color of the mixture will turn from clear to light amber to golden amber to slightly darker amber. Do not let it get too dark. Make sure you stand there and carefully watch the hot sugar mixture, because it will burn if you are not watching.

4. Remove the pan from the heat when the mixture turns darker amber and whisk in the butter and cream very slowly until it is melted and creamy. (The hot sugar will bubble like crazy when you start drizzling the cream in, but just keep whisking.)

5. Return the pan to the heat and let the caramel boil for 1 minute. Remove the pan from the heat and stir in the salt for salted caramel, if desired.

6. Let the caramel mixture cool before spooning it into a jar. Store the caramel in the refrigerator for up to one month. You may need to warm it up slightly in the microwave or let it come to room temperature before using it.

VARIATION:

For Caramel Topping: Use 4 tablespoons butter and 1⅓ cups whipping cream in the recipe.

Note. Put a tag on a mason jar of caramel and give it as a housewarming gift along with some apples.

Fruit Filling

PREP TIME: 5 MINUTES | **COOK TIME:** 10 MINUTES | **SERVING:** MAKES 1 CUP

Buying canned fruit filling is easy, but did you know that by just boiling fresh or frozen fruit down on the stove, you can get a fruit topping that doesn't have all those extra ingredients in it? I like to stir a little bit of honey into my fruit filling to give it a little sweeter taste and a silkier texture. Fruit filling is very versatile. You can put it on toast or in a Danish, or swirl it on top of a cheesecake!

INGREDIENTS

2 cups frozen fruit of your choice

2 tablespoons honey

INSTRUCTIONS

1. Place the frozen fruit in a saucepan and heat over medium-high heat until it thaws and comes to a boil.

2. Reduce the heat to low and simmer the fruit for 7 to 8 minutes, or until the juices cook off.

3. Stir in the honey and simmer for 1 to 2 minutes more.

4. Remove the pan from the heat and let the filling cool.

5. Store the filling in an airtight container in the refrigerator for up to 2 weeks.

Note. You can use fresh fruit in place of the frozen fruit. Just add 1 tablespoon water for each cup of fresh fruit in the saucepan.

Lemon Curd

PREP TIME: 10 MINUTES | COOK TIME: 10 MINUTES | SERVING: MAKES 1⅓ CUPS

Lemon curd is another one of those ingredients that I used to always buy from the store. Every recipe that I had ever seen called for so many egg yolks without the egg whites. I didn't want to find a recipe to use up all those extra egg whites I would have left over, so I never attempted any of those recipes. Then I realized that by using two whole eggs, I could have homemade lemon curd without any extra ingredients sitting around. The first time I made this, I couldn't wait to grab a spoon and dig in.

INGREDIENTS

1 cup sugar

1 teaspoon lemon zest

½ cup lemon juice, fresh or concentrate

½ cup (1 stick) unsalted butter

2 large eggs

INSTRUCTIONS

1. Stir together the sugar, lemon zest, lemon juice, and butter in a saucepan. Heat over low heat until everything is melted and smooth. Make sure to stir the mixture occasionally.

2. Whisk the eggs in a separate bowl until frothy. Very quickly, whisk ¼ cup of the hot sugar mixture into the eggs. Repeat with another ¼ cup of the sugar mixture.

3. Whisk the egg mixture into the remaining sugar mixture in the pan. Cook over medium heat, stirring continuously, for about 8 minutes. Do not let the mixture boil.

4. Pour the mixture through a fine-mesh strainer into a bowl to remove any lumps and strain out the zest. Use the back of a spoon to press the mixture through the strainer.

5. Place a piece of plastic wrap over the warm mixture, making sure it touches the entire surface of the lemon curd. Refrigerate until completely chilled. Store in an airtight container in the refrigerator for up to 2 weeks.

VARIATION:

For Blackberry Curd: Puree 1 cup fresh blackberries to get ½ cup puree. Use the puree in place of the lemon juice and leave out the lemon zest. Follow the rest of the instructions.

Apple Pie Filling

PREP TIME: 40 MINUTES | **COOK TIME:** 10 TO 12 MINUTES | **SERVING:** MAKES 4 CUPS

When my siblings and I were younger, we would visit my grandpa. He lived in a big farmhouse with an old horse barn. I can remember climbing all over the barn and playing hide and seek. On his property, he also had some apple trees. Put five children on a farm with apple trees and what do you get? Well, apple wars, of course. Rotten apple wars, that is. We would hide under the trees and throw the hard or rotten apples from the ground at one another. I have no idea who started it, but this game was so much fun, until you got hit with an apple. These days I prefer to enjoy my apples in a delicious pie filling instead of being hit in the head with them. This easy pie filling comes together in minutes and tastes amazing. Make sure you have enough time for the filling to cool and set up before you need to use it.

INGREDIENTS

6 cups diced peeled apples (any variety)

2 tablespoons lemon juice, fresh or concentrate

½ cup packed brown sugar

½ cup granulated sugar

¼ cup cornstarch

1 teaspoon ground cinnamon

¼ teaspoon ground nutmeg

¼ teaspoon salt

2 cups water

INSTRUCTIONS

1. Drizzle the lemon juice over the apples and toss to coat. Set the apples aside.

2. Stir together the sugars, cornstarch, cinnamon, nutmeg, and salt in a large saucepan. Whisk in the water until everything has dissolved.

3. Bring the mixture to a boil over medium-high heat. Reduce the heat slightly and simmer for 2 minutes.

4. Add the apples and increase the heat to medium-high heat to bring the mixture to a full boil again. Reduce the heat to low heat and simmer, stirring occasionally, for 10 to 12 minutes. Remove the pan from the heat and let the mixture cool.

5. Refrigerate the filling in an airtight container for 4 to 6 hours to thicken. Store in the refrigerator for up to 2 weeks.

Whipped Cream

PREP TIME: 30 MINUTES | **SERVING:** MAKES 2 CUPS

Making homemade whipped cream is easier than you may think. With two simple ingredients, you can have a fluffy topping that is perfect for garnishing the tops of cheesecakes. Make sure to chill the bowl and the wire whisk attachment ahead of time. This helps the cream whip up into stiff peaks faster.

INGREDIENTS

1 cup heavy cream
¼ cup powdered sugar

INSTRUCTIONS

1. Chill a metal bowl and mixer whisk attachment in the freezer for 30 minutes.

2. Pour the cream and powdered sugar into the chilled bowl.

3. Beat the mixture on high speed until stiff peaks form.

4. Store the whipped cream in an airtight container in the refrigerator for 3 to 4 days. Whip again briefly before serving.

VARIATION:

Vanilla Bean Whipped Cream: Add ½ teaspoon vanilla bean paste with the heavy cream and sugar.

Chocolate Whipped Cream: Add 1 tablespoon dark cocoa powder with the heavy cream and sugar.

Espresso Whipped Cream: Add 1 teaspoon espresso powder and 1 teaspoon cocoa powder with the heavy cream and sugar.

Toasted Coconut

PREP TIME: 2 MINUTES   COOK TIME: 5 MINUTES   SERVING: MAKES 1 CUP

Shredded coconut adds great taste and texture to baked goods. I am a fan of just grabbing a handful straight from the bag and munching on it while I am baking. Toasting the coconut adds crunch and nutty flavor that complement baked goods even more. It also fills your kitchen with the aroma of the tropics as it bakes.

INGREDIENTS

1 cup sweetened shredded coconut

INSTRUCTIONS

1. Preheat the oven to 350°F.

2. Spread the coconut out on a rimmed baking sheet. Bake for 4 to 5 minutes. Open the oven and stir the coconut every minute to ensure even coloring. It's okay if the heat escapes as you do this.

3. Remove the pan from the oven and let the coconut cool on the baking sheet.

4. Store the toasted coconut in an airtight container at room temperature for 2 weeks.

Cookie Dough

PREP TIME: 15 MINUTES

BAKE TIME: 12 MINUTES FOR COOKIES, 15 MINUTES FOR PIZZA

SERVING: MAKES 24 COOKIES OR 1 LARGE COOKIE PIZZA

This easy cookie dough is perfect for using in a variety of recipes. You can make small cookies, tarts, cookie pizzas, or bar cookies from this one dough. The possibilities for mix-ins are endless, too. Let your creativity run wild and have fun making cookies!

INGREDIENTS

½ cup (1 stick) unsalted butter, at room temperature

½ (4-ounce) package cream cheese, at room temperature

½ cup granulated sugar

¾ cup packed brown sugar

2 teaspoons vanilla extract

1 large egg

2½ cups all-purpose flour

½ teaspoon salt

1 teaspoon baking soda

INSTRUCTIONS

1. Preheat the oven to 375°F.

2. Beat the butter and cream cheese in a large bowl until creamy. Add the sugars and vanilla and beat again until smooth. Add the egg and beat again.

3. Stir together the flour, salt, and baking soda in a medium bowl. Slowly add the dry ingredients to the butter mixture until completely incorporated.

4. Roll the dough into 24 balls for cookies or press it out flat into a 12-inch circle for a cookie pizza.

5. Place the dough balls on a baking sheet a few inches apart and bake for 10 to 12 minutes. Or place the cookie pizza on a pizza pan and bake for 15 minutes.

1

Full-Size Cheesecakes

×

LARGER THAN LIFE!

Cheesecake is dangerous. Every time I open the refrigerator, I have to have one more bite, and then before you know it, I've eaten my entire weight in cheesecake. It's a dangerous and delicious thing. And full-size cheesecakes really are a work of baking art. They are a perfect showstopping dessert for parties, or even for a night of at-home indulgence!

Vanilla Bean Cheesecake

PREP TIME: 30 MINUTES | BAKE TIME: 1 HOUR 20 MINUTES | SERVING: MAKES ONE 10-INCH CHEESECAKE (14 SLICES)

Let's start simple, and what is more simple than vanilla? There is just something delicious about a slice of vanilla cheesecake piled high with strawberries, or any other topping, for that matter. By adding vanilla bean flecks and heavy cream into this cheesecake, simple vanilla becomes extraordinary. One of the best things about this easy cheesecake is that you can use it as a base to create so many other fun flavors.

INGREDIENTS

For the Crust

50 regular-size Nilla Wafer cookies

¼ cup sugar

6 tablespoons (¾ stick) unsalted butter, melted

For the Cheesecake

4 (8-ounce) packages cream cheese, at room temperature

1½ cups sugar

½ cup heavy cream

1 tablespoon vanilla bean paste

4 large eggs

1 batch Vanilla Bean Whipped Cream (page 29)

Fresh strawberries

INSTRUCTIONS

1. Place a large rimmed baking sheet on the very bottom rack of the oven and fill it halfway with water. Preheat the oven to 325°F. Line a 10-inch springform pan with parchment paper.

2. **For the Crust:** Pulse the cookies in a food processor a few times until they are completely crushed.

3. Mix together the cookie crumbs, sugar, and melted butter until it resembles coarse sand. Press the crumbs into the bottom of the prepared pan. Set aside.

4. Beat the cream cheese until creamy. Add the sugar and beat until smooth.

5. Add the cream and vanilla bean paste and beat until creamy.

6. Add the eggs one at a time, mixing well after each addition. Make sure the eggs are fully incorporated, but do not overbeat the batter.

7. Pour the cheesecake batter into the prepared crust. Place the pan on the oven rack right above the tray of water. Bake the cheesecake for 1 hour and 20 minutes.

(continued)

8. Remove the cheesecake from the oven and place it on a wire rack. Let cool for 5 minutes, then run a sharp knife around the edges of the cheese-cake to loosen it from the pan.

9. Let the cheesecake cool for 1 hour, then refrigerate it for 4 to 6 hours, or until completely chilled. Detach the springform pan ring and remove the cheesecake from the pan. Slide the cheesecake onto a serving plate.

10. Serve with Vanilla Bean Whipped Cream and fresh strawberries, if desired.

Banana Split Cheesecake

PREP TIME: 40 MINUTES | **BAKE TIME:** 1 HOUR 40 MINUTES | **SERVING:** MAKES ONE 10-INCH CHEESECAKE (14 SLICES)

Throughout college, I waitressed at a restaurant in the local mall during the school break. Our goal was not only to help the customer enjoy their dinner, but to encourage them to order ice cream as well. After all, there is always room for ice cream, right? The restaurant had a variety of different sundaes, but my favorite one to make was the banana split ice cream sundae. Banana split lovers everywhere are going to go crazy over this gorgeous cheesecake because it incorporates almost everything about that traditional ice cream dessert in each creamy bite. Banana, chocolate, and strawberry make this cheesecake a great dessert to make for fancy dinners. Add swirls of whipped cream and cherries on top and it is truly a dessert showstopper!

INGREDIENTS

For the Crust

2 cups graham cracker crumbs

¼ cup sugar

6 tablespoons unsalted butter, melted

For the Cheesecake

4 (8-ounce) packages cream cheese, at room temperature

1 cup sugar

1 tablespoon vanilla extract

1 cup mashed ripe banana

¼ cup all-purpose flour

4 large eggs

1 (21-ounce) can strawberry pie filling

INSTRUCTIONS

1. Place a large rimmed baking sheet on the very bottom rack of the oven and fill it halfway with water. Preheat the oven to 325°F. Line a 10-inch springform pan with parchment paper.

2. **For the Crust:** Mix together the graham cracker crumbs, sugar, and melted butter. Press the crumbs into the bottom of the prepared pan. Set aside.

3. **For the Cheesecake:** Beat the cream cheese until creamy. Add the sugar and vanilla and beat until smooth.

4. Add the banana and flour and beat until incorporated.

5. Add the eggs one at a time, mixing well after each addition. Make sure the eggs are fully incorporated, but do not overbeat the batter.

6. Pour the cheesecake batter into the prepared crust. Spoon dollops of pie filling randomly over the top of the cheesecake batter. Gently use a butter knife to swirl the cheesecake and filling together.

(continued)

Banana Split Cheesecake (continued)

For the Topping

½ cup heavy cream

1 cup chocolate chips

1 batch Whipped Cream
(page 29; optional)

Cherries with stems (optional)

Walnuts (optional)

7. Place the cheesecake on the oven rack right above the tray of water. Bake the cheesecake for 1 hour and 40 minutes.

8. Remove the cheesecake from the oven and place it on a wire rack. Let cool for 5 minutes, then run a sharp knife around the edges of the cheesecake to loosen it from the pan.

9. Let the cheesecake cool for 1 hour, then refrigerate it for 4 to 6 hours, or until it is completely chilled.

10. Detach the springform pan ring and remove the cheesecake from the pan. Slide the cheesecake onto a serving plate.

11. **For the Topping:** Place the cream and chocolate chips in a microwave-safe bowl. Microwave for 30 seconds. Stir the chocolate until melted and creamy. Heat for an additional 15 seconds, if needed.

12. Pour the chocolate over the top of the cheesecake. Spread the chocolate to the edges of the cheesecake with an offset spatula. Refrigerate the cheesecake until the chocolate is set. Top with whipped cream, cherries, and walnuts, if desired.

Lemon Cheesecake

PREP TIME: 40 MINUTES | BAKE TIME: 60 TO 65 MINUTES | SERVING: MAKES ONE 9-INCH CHEESECAKE (12 SLICES)

I didn't used to like lemon desserts. I usually would head straight for the chocolate. Forget those fruity desserts. Momma wants her chocolate! But for some strange reason, lemon desserts have become more enjoyable to me as I've gotten older. Lemon has such a fresh, springlike flavor. It must be true that your taste buds mature as you get older. This mild and creamy lemon cheesecake gets a citrus blast from the homemade lemon curd and fresh berries on top. I can't get enough of this fruity cheesecake!

INGREDIENTS

For the Crust

2 cups gingersnap cookie crumbs

¼ cup sugar

6 tablespoons unsalted butter, melted

For the Cheesecake

3 (8-ounce) packages cream cheese, at room temperature

1½ cups sugar

½ cup sour cream

⅓ cup lemon juice, fresh or concentrate

Zest of 1 lemon

¼ cup all-purpose flour

3 large eggs

For the Topping

1 batch Lemon Curd (page 27)

Fresh fruit

INSTRUCTIONS

1. Preheat the oven to 350°F. Line a 9-inch springform pan with parchment paper.

2. **For the Crust:** Mix together the cookie crumbs, sugar, and butter. Press the crumbs firmly into the bottom of the prepared pan. Bake for 10 minutes. Remove the pan from the oven and let the crust cool. Keep the oven on.

3. Place a large rimmed baking sheet on the very bottom rack of the oven and fill it halfway with water.

4. **For the Cheesecake:** Beat the cream cheese until creamy. Add the sugar and sour cream and beat the mixture again.

5. Add the lemon zest, lemon juice, and flour and beat until incorporated.

6. Add the eggs one at a time, beating after each addition. Make sure the eggs are fully incorporated, but do not overbeat the mixture.

7. Pour the cheesecake batter into the cooled crust. Place the pan on the oven rack above the tray of water. Bake the cheesecake for 50 to 55 minutes.

8. Remove the pan from the oven and place it on a wire

rack. Let cool for 5 minutes, then run a sharp knife around the edge of the cheesecake to loosen it from the springform pan. Let the cheesecake cool for 1 hour, then refrigerate it for 4 to 6 hours, or until completely chilled.

9. Detach the springform pan ring and remove the cheesecake from the pan. Slide it onto a serving plate.

10. For the Topping: Spread the lemon curd on the top of the cheesecake with an offset spatula. Refrigerate the cheesecake for 1 hour more. Place fresh fruit on top immediately before serving.

Frozen Mint Cookie Crumble Cheesecake

PREP TIME: 30 MINUTES PLUS FREEZE TIME | **SERVING:** MAKES ONE 9-INCH CHEESECAKE (12 SLICES)

Growing up, I didn't really like ice cream. Yes, I know. What was wrong with me? I think it was just too cold, or I was just too busy eating brownies and Oatmeal Crème Pies. But my daughter absolutely loves ice cream, and this fun frozen cheesecake was inspired by her love for mint chocolate chip ice cream. There is no shortage of mint and chocolate going on in here. Plenty of cookies and chocolate chips have been scattered throughout the creamy mint goodness, and then even more cookies have been piled on top just waiting for you to grab a spoon and dig in. This creation will be sure to tame the ice cream cookie monster in your home.

INGREDIENTS

For the Crust

30 chocolate mint Grasshopper cookies

4 tablespoons (½ stick) unsalted butter, melted

For the Cheesecake

1½ cups heavy cream

1 (8-ounce) package cream cheese, at room temperature

1 (14-ounce) can sweetened condensed milk

1 teaspoon mint extract

Green gel food coloring

15 chocolate mint Grasshopper cookies

¼ cup mini chocolate chips

For the Topping

¼ cup hot fudge topping

1 cup Whipped Cream (page 29)

7 Grasshopper cookies

INSTRUCTIONS

1. For the Crust: Line a 9-inch springform pan with parchment paper. Place the cookies in a food processor and pulse until they are crushed to crumbs.

2. Mix together the cookie crumbs and melted butter. Press the crumbs firmly and evenly into the bottom of the prepared pan. Place the pan in the freezer while you make the cheesecake.

3. For the Cheesecake: Beat the heavy cream until stiff peaks form. Set the whipped cream aside.

4. Beat the cream cheese until creamy. Slowly add the condensed milk and mint extract and beat again until creamy. You may need to use a wire whisk attachment to get the mixture smooth.

5. Fold in the whipped cream with a rubber spatula until everything is mixed together. Add a little bit of green gel food coloring with a toothpick, a little bit at a time. Continue adding and stirring until you reach a mint color you like.

(continued)

6. Chop the cookies into large crumbs, and then gently stir the cookie chunks and mini chocolate chips into the cheesecake batter.

7. Spoon the cheesecake mixture on top of the prepared crust. Freeze the cheesecake for at least 6 hours.

8. Run a knife under very hot water, dry it off, and then run it around the edge of the cheesecake to loosen it from the springform pan. Detach the springform pan ring from the cheesecake and slide the cheesecake onto a serving plate.

9. <u>**For the Topping:**</u> Warm the hot fudge in the microwave for 15 to 20 seconds. Drizzle the hot fudge over the top of the cheesecake. Chop the cookies into chunks and sprinkle them on top of the cheesecake.

10. Pipe swirls of whipped cream around the edges of the cheesecake using a piping bag and icing tip 1M. Top the swirls with extra mint chocolate cookies, if desired. Keep frozen.

Raspberry Fudge Cheesecake

PREP TIME: 30 MINUTES | BAKE TIME: 1 HOUR 30 MINUTES | SERVING: MAKES ONE 10-INCH CHEESECAKE (14 SLICES)

Swirls of raspberry pie filling and hot fudge will hypnotize you as you stare down this cheesecake. I made this cheesecake for a party right after we moved to a new town. Everyone was impressed with the creaminess and swirls of this gorgeous cheesecake. I have to admit that it felt pretty good to watch the entire cheesecake disappear in under 10 minutes. Let's just say my new friends decided to keep me around for a while.

INGREDIENTS

For the Crust

20 Oreo cookies

4 tablespoons (½ stick) unsalted butter, melted

For the Cheesecake

4 (8-ounce) packages cream cheese, at room temperature

1½ cups sugar

½ cup heavy cream

2 teaspoons almond extract

¼ cup all-purpose flour

4 large eggs

¾ cup hot fudge topping

1 cup raspberry pie filling (page 26)

Fresh raspberries

INSTRUCTIONS

1. Place a large rimmed baking sheet on the bottom rack of the oven and fill it halfway with water. Preheat the oven to 325°F. Line a 10-inch springform pan with parchment paper.

2. **For the Crust:** Place the cookies, cream filling included, in a food processor and pulse until they are crushed into crumbs.

3. Mix together the cookie crumbs and butter. Press the crumbs evenly and firmly into the bottom of the prepared pan. Set aside.

4. **For the Cheesecake:** Beat the cream cheese until creamy. Add the sugar and beat until completely mixed and smooth.

5. Add the heavy cream, almond extract, and flour. Beat until incorporated.

6. Add the eggs one at a time, beating after each addition. Make sure the eggs are fully incorporated, but do not overbeat the batter. Pour the cheesecake batter into the prepared pan.

(continued)

7. Heat the hot fudge for 15 to 20 seconds or until pourable. Drop the hot fudge and pie filling randomly over the top of the cheesecake batter. Gently use a knife to swirl the top of the batter. Make sure you do not go all the way through to the crust with the knife.

8. Place the pan in the oven on the oven rack right above the tray of water. Bake for 1 hour and 30 minutes.

9. Remove the cheesecake from the oven and place it on a wire rack. Let the cheesecake cool for 5 minutes, then run a sharp knife around the edge of the cheesecake to loosen it from the springform pan. Let the cheesecake cool for 1 hour, then refrigerate it for 4 to 6 hours, or until completely chilled.

10. Detach the ring on the springform pan carefully and remove the cheesecake. Slide the cheesecake onto a serving plate. Serve with fresh raspberries on top.

Strawberry Chocolate Cheesecake

PREP TIME: 35 MINUTES | **BAKE TIME:** 40 MINUTES | **SERVING:** MAKES ONE 9-INCH CHEESECAKE (12 SLICES)

My husband and I created this fun cheesecake together a few years ago for the blog. One of his favorite desserts is a strawberry pie that his mom made when he was growing up. As you should know by now, my favorite dessert is cheesecake. In marriage, we became one. So naturally, our two favorite desserts had to become one, and it was an exciting day when they got transformed into one happy cheesecake mash-up. His love of strawberry pie was layered on top of my chocolate cheesecake love. Not knowing how it was going to turn out, we held our breath as we opened the pan. Would the strawberry layer stay on the cheesecake? We both did a dance of joy when we opened the pan ring and saw that it was a success!

INGREDIENTS

For the Crust

20 Oreo cookies

4 tablespoons (½ stick) unsalted butter, melted

For the Chocolate Cheesecake

1½ cups semisweet chocolate chips

1 (8-ounce) package cream cheese, at room temperature

2 tablespoons heavy cream

½ teaspoon vanilla extract

2 large eggs

For the Vanilla Cheesecake

2 (8-ounce) packages cream cheese, at room temperature

1 cup sugar

1 cup sour cream

1 tablespoon vanilla extract

2 large eggs

INSTRUCTIONS

1. Place a large rimmed baking sheet on the very bottom rack of the oven and fill it halfway with water. Preheat the oven to 350°F. Line a 10-inch springform pan with parchment paper.

2. **For the Crust:** Place the cookies, cream filling included, in a food processor. Pulse the cookies until they become crumbs.

3. Mix the cookie crumbs and melted butter together. Press the crumbs evenly in the bottom of the prepared pan.

4. **For the Chocolate Cheesecake:** Place the chocolate chips in a small saucepan. Heat over low heat until melted and creamy. Remove the pan from the heat.

5. Cut the cream cheese into cubes. Add to the melted chocolate and stir until the mixture is melted and creamy.

6. Stir in the cream and vanilla until smooth. Add the eggs one at a time and whisk until incorporated.

(continued)

For the Strawberry Pie

1¼ cups water

¾ cup sugar

2 tablespoons cornstarch

1 (3-ounce) box strawberry Jell-O

4 cups sliced strawberries

7. Pour the cheesecake batter onto the prepared crust. Set aside.

8. **For the Vanilla Cheesecake:** Beat the cream cheese until creamy. Add the sugar and beat the mixture until smooth.

9. Add the sour cream and vanilla and beat again.

10. Add the eggs one at a time, mixing well after each addition. Make sure the eggs are fully incorporated, but do not overbeat the batter.

11. Spoon the vanilla cheesecake batter evenly on top of the chocolate cheesecake batter in the pan.

12. Place the pan in the oven on the rack right above the tray of water. Bake the cheesecake for 45 to 48 minutes.

13. Remove the pan from the oven and place it on a wire rack. Do not run a knife around the top of this cheesecake. We want the cheesecake to stay tight to the pan, so the Jell-O layer doesn't leak down the sides.

14. Let the cheesecake cool for 1 hour, then refrigerate it for 4 to 5 hours to cool completely.

15. **For the Strawberry Pie:** Whisk together the water, sugar, and cornstarch in a saucepan. Bring the mixture to a boil over high heat. Reduce the heat to maintain a simmer and cook for 2 minutes.

16. Remove the pan from the heat and whisk in the Jell-O powder. Stir until it has dissolved. Set the pan aside to cool for at least 30 minutes.

17. Layer the sliced strawberries on top of the chilled cheesecake. Pour the cooled Jell-O on top of the berries evenly. Place the pan in the refrigerator and chill for 2 to 3 hours more, or until everything is set. Serve with cool whip, if desired.

White Chocolate–Blackberry Cheesecake

PREP TIME: 45 MINUTES | **BAKE TIME:** 65 MINUTES | **SERVING:** MAKES ONE 9-INCH CHEESECAKE (12 SLICES)

I have many fond memories from growing up, and you'll discover that most of them revolve around food. I remember climbing the little hills beside our country road with my brother and sisters, picking fresh raspberries and blackberries. We would walk the entire road trying to fill an old ice cream bucket with those berries. Many of those warm berries never actually made it back to the house because we would eat them as fast as we picked them. As I stirred the blackberries into this creamy white chocolate cheesecake batter, I could not help but be transported back in time to that dusty dirt road. It's wonderful how food can trigger memories from your childhood and make you smile.

INGREDIENTS

For the Cookie Dough Crust

4 tablespoons (½ stick) unsalted butter

¼ cup vegetable shortening

⅓ cup brown sugar

2 teaspoons molasses

½ teaspoon vanilla extract

1 large egg

¾ cup all-purpose flour

¼ teaspoon salt

1 teaspoon ground cinnamon

¾ cup quick-cooking oats

For the Cheesecake

3 (8-ounce) packages cream cheese, at room temperature

1 cup granulated sugar

1 cup sour cream

1 teaspoon vanilla extract

INSTRUCTIONS

1. Preheat the oven to 350°F. Line a 9-inch springform pan with parchment paper.

2. **For the Cookie Dough Crust:** Beat the butter, shortening, and sugar until creamy. Add the molasses, vanilla, and egg and beat until incorporated.

3. Stir together the flour, salt, cinnamon, and oats in a bowl. Slowly add the dry ingredients to the butter mixture until everything is incorporated.

4. Press the cookie dough evenly into the bottom of the prepared pan.

5. Bake the crust for 10 minutes. Remove the pan from the oven and let cool on a wire rack. Do not remove the springform pan ring. Leave the oven on.

6. Place a large rimmed baking sheet on the very bottom rack of the oven and fill it halfway with water.

8 ounces white baking chocolate, melted

¼ cup plus 1 tablespoon all-purpose flour

3 large eggs

3 cups fresh blackberries

For the Topping

1 batch Blackberry Curd (page 27)

1 cup fresh blackberries

Fresh mint leaves, if desired

7. For the Cheesecake: Beat the cream cheese until creamy. Add the sugar, sour cream, and vanilla and beat until smooth.

8. Spoon the melted white chocolate into the mixture and beat until incorporated. Add ¼ cup of the flour and beat again.

9. Add the eggs one at a time, mixing well after each addition. Make sure the eggs are fully incorporated, but do not overbeat the batter.

10. Toss the blackberries with the remaining 1 tablespoon flour. Gently fold the berries into the cheesecake batter. Pour the cheesecake mixture onto the cooled crust. Place the pan on the oven rack right above the tray of water. Bake the cheesecake for 55 minutes.

11. Remove the pan from the oven and let the cheesecake cool for 5 minutes. Run a sharp knife around the edges of the cheesecake to loosen it from the springform pan. Let the cheesecake cool for 1 hour, then refrigerate it for 4 to 6 hours, or until completely chilled.

12. Detach the springform pan ring and remove the cheesecake from the pan. Slide the cheesecake onto a serving plate.

13. For the Topping: Top the cheesecake with the blackberry curd and refrigerate for 1 hour. Right before serving, add fresh blackberries and mint leaves to the top. Sprinkle with powdered sugar, if desired.

Triple Chocolate Mousse Cheesecake

PREP TIME: 45 MINUTES | **BAKE TIME:** 45 MINUTES | **SERVING:** MAKES ONE 9-INCH CHEESECAKE (12 SLICES)

A friend of our family inspired this fun layered chocolate cheesecake. Pastor Jim, as all the kids at church fondly call him, absolutely loves chocolate cheesecake. Every year when the mission's dessert auction would come up, he would nudge me and ask if there would be a cheesecake for him to bid on. I think he would bid on any cheesecake flavor, to be honest, but I know chocolate is his favorite. The last auction that we attended, I made this chocolate cheesecake with him in mind. And sure enough, he outbid everyone. Three layers of different chocolate make this cheesecake perfect for when you need that chocolate fix.

INGREDIENTS

For the Crust

20 Oreo cookies

4 tablespoons (½ stick) unsalted butter, melted

For the Cheesecake

2 (8-ounce) packages cream cheese, at room temperature

⅔ cup sugar

⅔ cup sour cream

1½ teaspoons vanilla extract

4 ounces bittersweet baking chocolate, melted

¼ cup all-purpose flour

2 large eggs

For the Mousse

1 (8-ounce) cream cheese, at room temperature

1 teaspoon vanilla extract

INSTRUCTIONS

1. Place a large rimmed baking sheet on the very bottom rack of the oven and fill it halfway with water. Preheat the oven to 350°F. Line a 9-inch springform pan with parchment paper.

2. **For the Crust:** Place the cookies, cream filling included, in a food processor. Pulse until the cookies are crushed into crumbs.

3. Mix together the cookie crumbs and butter. Press the crumbs evenly into the bottom of the prepared pan. Set aside.

4. **For the Cheesecake:** Beat the cream cheese until creamy. Add the sugar, sour cream, and vanilla and beat until very smooth.

5. Spoon in the melted chocolate and beat until incorporated completely. Add the flour and beat again.

(continued)

4 ounces white baking chocolate, melted

1 (8-ounce) container Cool Whip, thawed

For the Topping

2 tablespoons heavy cream

¼ cup chocolate chips

6. Add the eggs one at a time, beating well after each addition. Make sure the eggs are fully incorporated, but do not overbeat the batter.

7. Pour the cheesecake batter onto the prepared crust. Place the pan on the oven rack right above the pan of water. Bake the cheesecake for 45 minutes.

8. Remove the pan from the oven and place it on a wire rack. Let the cheesecake cool for 5 minutes, then run a sharp knife around the edges of the cheesecake to loosen it from the springform pan.

9. Let the cheesecake cool for 1 hour, then refrigerate it for 4 to 6 hours, or until completely chilled.

10. Detach the springform pan ring and gently remove the cheesecake from the pan. Slide the cheesecake onto a plate.

11. **For the Mousse:** Beat the cream cheese and vanilla until creamy. Spoon in the melted white chocolate and beat the mixture until smooth.

12. Fold in the Cool Whip with a rubber spatula until everything is completely mixed together. Pipe the mousse on top of the chilled cheesecake with a piping bag and icing tip 1M. Refrigerate the cheesecake for one hour to let it set up.

13. **For the Topping:** Place the cream and chocolate chips in a microwave-safe bowl and microwave for 15 to 20 seconds. Stir the chocolate until melted and creamy. Drizzle the chocolate over the top of the cheesecake.

Pumpkin Chai Cheesecake

PREP TIME: 40 MINUTES | BAKE TIME: 1 HOUR 40 MINUTES | SERVING: MAKES ONE 9-INCH CHEESECAKE (12 SLICES)

Pumpkin pie is a staple at most Thanksgiving tables. While I enjoy holiday traditions, I also love putting a special twist to make that holiday even more memorable. Most days I enjoy a cup of coffee in the afternoon, but every once in a while I change that up and have a hot chai tea. One afternoon after enjoying a chai latte, I realized that those spices were the perfect complement to a pumpkin dessert. For this cheesecake, I took the pumpkin out of the pie and added it to a creamy cheesecake loaded with different spices. Pumpkin pie is good, but Pumpkin Chai Cheesecake will make your holiday dessert stand out!

INGREDIENTS

For the Crust

1½ cups graham cracker crumbs

¼ cup granulated sugar

6 tablespoons (¾ stick) unsalted butter, melted

For the Cheesecake

4 (8-ounce) packages cream cheese, at room temperature

1 cup packed brown sugar

½ cup granulated sugar

¼ cup heavy cream

1 (15-ounce) can pumpkin puree

1 tablespoon vanilla extract

¼ cup all-purpose flour

1 tablespoon ground cinnamon

1 teaspoon ground nutmeg

½ teaspoon ground cloves

½ teaspoon ground ginger

½ teaspoon ground cardamom

½ teaspoon ground star anise

4 large eggs

INSTRUCTIONS

1. Place a large rimmed baking sheet on the very bottom rack of the oven and fill it halfway with water. Preheat the oven to 325°F. Line a 9-inch springform pan with parchment paper.

2. **For the Crust:** Mix together the graham cracker crumbs, granulated sugar, and melted butter. Press the crumbs evenly on the bottom of the prepared pan. Set aside.

3. **For the Cheesecake:** Beat the cream cheese until creamy. Add the sugars, cream, pumpkin, and vanilla and beat until everything is thoroughly mixed.

4. Stir together the flour and spices. Add to the mixture and beat again.

5. Add the eggs one at a time, beating well after each addition. Make sure the eggs are fully incorporated, but do not overbeat the batter.

6. Pour the cheesecake batter onto the prepared crust. Place the pan on the oven rack right above the tray of water. Bake the cheesecake for 1 hour and 35 minutes.

(continued)

Pumpkin Chai Cheesecake (continued)

For the Topping

2 cups sour cream

¼ cup granulated sugar

1 teaspoon ground cinnamon

½ teaspoon ground nutmeg

½ teaspoon ground ginger

¼ teaspoon ground cloves

¼ teaspoon ground star anise

1 cup Whipped Cream (page 29)

7. **For the Topping:** Whisk together the sour cream, granulated sugar, and spices until smooth.

8. Remove the cheesecake from the oven and spread the sour cream mixture evenly on top with an offset spatula. Place the pan back in the oven and bake the cheesecake for 5 minutes more.

9. Remove the cheesecake from the oven and place the pan on a wire rack. Let the cheesecake cool for 5 minutes, then run a sharp knife around the edge of the cheesecake to loosen it from the springform pan.

10. Let the cheesecake cool for 1 hour, then refrigerate it for 4 to 6 hours, or until completely chilled.

11. Detach the springform pan ring and remove the cheesecake from the pan. Slide the cheesecake onto a serving plate. Sprinkle with extra spices, if desired.

12. Pipe swirls of whipped cream around the edges of the cheesecake using a piping bag and icing tip 1M.

Marshmallow S'mores Cheesecake

PREP TIME: 1 HOUR | **BAKE TIME:** 50 MINUTES | **SERVING:** MAKES ONE 9-INCH CHEESECAKE (12 SLICES)

Growing up, we always made campfires and toasted marshmallows when we went camping. I never realized how much of a chaotic mess this activity was until we had our own kids. There are always sticks and flaming marshmallows flying all over the place. Because let's be honest, our kids don't patiently roast a marshmallow. Their idea of "roasting" is to ignite their marshmallow in the hot coals and then pretend to be Indiana Jones with their flaming sugar ball torches—not to mention the sticky mess that ends up all over the place. Adding s'mores flair to baked goods helps me enjoy that same flavor in our kitchen without the fire craziness. A buttery graham cracker crust pairs perfectly with a creamy marshmallow cheesecake, and then everything is completely covered in chocolate. We could stop there, but why not keep going? Adding a soft fluffy marshmallow meringue frosting that is toasted finishes off the s'mores effect. This was one cheesecake I definitely could not wait to dig into!

INGREDIENTS

For the Crust

2 cups graham cracker crumbs

¼ cup sugar

½ cup (1 stick) unsalted butter, melted

For the Cheesecake

3 (8-ounce) packages cream cheese, at room temperature

¾ cup sugar

½ cup sour cream

1 teaspoon vanilla extract

1 (7-ounce) jar marshmallow crème

3 large eggs

INSTRUCTIONS

1. Place a large rimmed baking sheet on the very bottom rack of the oven and fill it halfway with water. Preheat the oven to 350°F. Line a 9-inch springform pan with parchment paper.

2. <u>For the Crust:</u> Mix together the graham cracker crumbs, sugar, and melted butter. Press the crumbs evenly into the bottom of the prepared pan. Set aside.

3. <u>For the Cheesecake:</u> Beat the cream cheese until creamy. Add the sugar and sour cream and beat until smooth.

4. Add the vanilla and marshmallow crème and beat until everything is incorporated completely.

(continued)

For the Topping

½ cup heavy cream

1 cup chocolate chips

4 full-size (1.55 ounce) Hershey's chocolate bars, broken apart

For the Meringue Frosting

3 large egg whites

¾ cup sugar

¼ teaspoon cream of tartar

½ teaspoon vanilla extract

5. Add the eggs one at a time, beating well after each addition. Make sure the eggs are fully incorporated, but do not overbeat the batter.

6. Pour the cheesecake batter onto the prepared crust. Place the pan on the oven rack right above the tray of water. Bake for 50 minutes.

7. Remove the pan from the oven and place it on a wire rack. Let the cheesecake cool for 5 minutes and then run a sharp knife around the edge of the cheesecake to loosen it from the springform pan.

8. Let the cheesecake cool for 1 hour, then refrigerate it for 4 to 6 hours, or until completely chilled.

9. **For the Topping:** Place the cream and chocolate chips in a microwave-safe bowl. Microwave for 15 to 30 seconds. Stir until the chocolate is melted and creamy. Let the chocolate cool slightly.

10. Detach the springform pan ring and remove the cheesecake from the pan. Slide it off the parchment paper back onto the bottom of the springform pan.

11. Place the cheesecake on a wire rack with a baking sheet underneath. Pour the melted chocolate in the middle of the cheesecake. Use an offset spatula to slowly spread the chocolate over the top and down the sides of the cheesecake. The entire cheesecake should be covered with chocolate. Place the cheesecake, pan, and wire rack in the refrigerator for 10 to 15 minutes.

12. Lift the cheesecake off the wire rack and place it on a serving plate. Place the Hershey's bars around the very bottom of the cheesecake, pressing them into the soft chocolate coating. Refrigerate the cheesecake again until the chocolate is completely set.

13. <u>For the Meringue Frosting:</u> Place the egg whites, sugar, and cream of tartar in a heatproof bowl. Set the bowl directly over a saucepan of simmering water. Make sure the bowl does not touch the water. Whisk the mixture for 5 to 6 minutes, or until the sugar has dissolved and the egg whites are warm to the touch.

14. Beat the mixture with a whisk attachment for 6 to 8 minutes, or until stiff, glossy peaks form. Gently stir in the vanilla.

15. Spread the meringue topping on top of the cheesecake. Use an offset spatula to create peaks.

16. Use a kitchen torch to lightly toast the meringue frosting. Refrigerate the cheesecake until ready to serve.

Coconut Cream Cheesecake

PREP TIME: 30 MINUTES | **BAKE TIME:** 55 TO 60 MINUTES | **SERVING:** MAKES ONE 9-INCH CHEESECAKE (12 SLICES)

One of my favorite candy bars is a Mounds Bar. I love that creamy coconut center that is covered in dark chocolate. Unfortunately, my love of coconut has not transferred to our kids. I keep trying to hide it in baked goods, but they find it and give me dirty looks. I guess that just means more coconut goodness for me! I wanted this cheesecake to be similar to the Mounds Bar, so I kept it pretty simple. The creamy coconut cheesecake with a dark chocolate coating totally satisfied my candy bar longings.

INGREDIENTS

For the Crust

20 Oreo cookies

4 tablespoons (½ stick) unsalted butter, melted

For the Cheesecake

3 (8-ounce) packages cream cheese, at room temperature

1 cup sugar

¼ cup sour cream

½ cup cream of coconut

1 teaspoon coconut extract

3 large eggs

1 cup sweetened shredded coconut

For the Topping

¾ cup dark chocolate chips

¼ cup heavy cream

1 batch Whipped Cream (page 29)

4 or 5 chocolate coconut candy bars, cut in half (optional)

INSTRUCTIONS

1. Place a large rimmed baking sheet on the very bottom rack of the oven and fill it halfway with water. Preheat the oven to 350°F. Line a 9-inch springform pan with parchment paper.

2. **For the Crust:** Place the cookies, cream filling included, in a food processor. Pulse until the cookies are crumbs.

3. Mix together the cookie crumbs and melted butter. Press the crumbs evenly into the bottom of the prepared pan. Set aside.

4. **For the Cheesecake:** Beat the cream cheese until creamy. Add the sugar and beat until smooth.

5. Add the sour cream, cream of coconut, and coconut extract and beat until creamy again.

6. Add the eggs one at a time, beating well after each addition. Make sure the eggs are fully incorporated, but do not overbeat the mixture.

7. Gently stir in the shredded coconut. Pour the cheesecake batter onto the prepared crust. Place the pan on the oven rack right above the tray of water. Bake for 55 to 60 minutes.

(continued)

8. Remove the pan from the oven and place it on a wire rack. Let the cheesecake cool for 5 minutes. Run a sharp knife around the edges of the cheesecake to loosen it from the sides of the springform pan.

9. Let the cheesecake cool for 1 hour, then refrigerate it for 4 to 6 hours, or until completely chilled.

10. Detach the springform pan ring and gently remove the cheesecake. Slide the cheesecake onto a serving plate.

11. For the Topping: Place the chocolate chips and cream in a microwave-safe bowl. Microwave for 30 seconds. Stir the mixture until creamy. If needed, heat for another 15 seconds.

12. Pour the chocolate in the center of the chilled cheesecake and spread it out using an offset spatula. Gently spread the chocolate to the edge of the cheesecake, letting a small amount drip down the sides.

13. Pipe the whipped cream around the edge of the cheesecake using a piping bag and icing tip 1M. Top the swirls with candy bar pieces, if desired.

Note. If you like almonds, sprinkle ½ cup sliced almonds onto the chocolate topping before it sets.

Caramel Pecan Cheesecake

PREP TIME: 30 MINUTES | BAKE TIME: 60 MINUTES | SERVING: MAKES ONCE 9-INCH CHEESECAKE (12 SLICES)

I like to bring the extra desserts I make every week to the Wednesday-night dinner we attend at our church. Most of these nights, our family brings the desserts in before everyone else gets there. One night, I was running a little bit behind, so we walked in ten minutes late. You should have seen everyone jump up from his or her seats and hover around us as we set the desserts on the food table. This caramel cheesecake did not have a chance at surviving. It disappeared within minutes of being set down. Believe me, I was so glad I had saved a piece at home to enjoy later! This creamy caramel cheesecake paired with a gooey caramel and pecan topping will have your taste buds begging for more! You will not regret making it.

INGREDIENTS

For the Crust

1½ cups graham cracker crumbs

¼ cup granulated sugar

6 tablespoons (¾ stick) unsalted butter, melted

For the Cheesecake

4 (8-ounce) packages cream cheese, at room temperature

1½ cups packed brown sugar

¼ cup heavy cream

¼ cup Caramel Topping (page 25)

1 teaspoon vanilla extract

1 teaspoon caramel extract

¼ cup all-purpose flour

4 large eggs

For the Topping

½ cup finely chopped pecans

1 batch Caramel Dip (page 24)

INSTRUCTIONS

1. Place a large rimmed baking sheet on the very bottom rack of the oven and fill it halfway with water. Preheat the oven to 350°F. Line a 9-inch springform pan with parchment paper.

2. **For the Crust:** Mix together the graham cracker crumbs, sugar, and butter. Press the crumbs firmly into the bottom of the prepared pan. Set aside.

3. **For the Cheesecake:** Beat the cream cheese until creamy. Add the brown sugar and beat until smooth.

4. Pour in the cream, caramel topping, extracts, and flour. Beat until everything is incorporated completely.

5. Add the eggs one at a time, beating well after each addition. Make sure the eggs are fully incorporated, but do not overbeat the batter.

6. Pour the cheesecake mixture onto the prepared crust. Place the pan on the oven rack right above the tray of water. Bake for 60 minutes.

7. Remove the pan from the oven and place it on a wire rack. Let the cheesecake cool for five minutes, then run a sharp knife around the edge of the cheesecake to loosen it from the springform pan.

8. Let the cheesecake cool for 1 hour, then refrigerate it for 4 to 6 hours, or until completely chilled.

9. Detach the springform pan ring and remove the cheesecake from the pan. Slide it onto a serving plate.

10. <u>**For the Topping:**</u> Stir the pecans into the caramel dip. Spread this mixture on top of the cheesecake right before serving.

Note. If you refrigerate this cheesecake with the caramel dip on top, the caramel will harden. Run a sharp knife under very hot water. Dry it off and very slowly cut through the caramel so that you do not crush the soft cheesecake. The hot knife will melt the caramel as you cut through.

2

Cheesecake Cupcakes

×

SMALL WONDERS

Cheesecake does not have to be huge to be delicious. Did you know that any cheesecake recipe could be baked into little individual portions? Talk about dangerous information, right? These bite-size treats are more manageable for everyday eating or sharing, so you won't have the temptation of a full-size cheesecake in your fridge! Although if you are anything like me, eating five mini cheesecakes in one day wouldn't be that hard to do.

Banana Caramel Cheesecakes

PREP TIME: 2 HOURS 25 MINUTES | BAKE TIME: 23 TO 25 MINUTES | SERVING: MAKES 12 MINI CHEESECAKES

Bananas are a hit-or-miss item for me. I can only eat them if they are green and crunch like an apple. Once they turn yellow, I will not touch them with a ten-foot pole, and the bananas sit on the counter until they turn brown. At that point, no one else in the house is going to touch them, either. Luckily, I absolutely love to bake with bananas. So I get excited when those bananas are still there, and I have a fun recipe idea to try out. Here I took the Banana Split Cheesecake from page 37 and condensed it down into bite-size cheesecakes. Adding my beloved caramel dip to the top of these little cheesecakes was a fun way to change them up. Go ahead. Try them. You will not be disappointed!

INGREDIENTS

For the Crust

¾ cup graham cracker crumbs

1 tablespoon sugar

3 tablespoons unsalted butter, melted

For the Cheesecake

2 (8-ounce) packages cream cheese, at room temperature

½ cup sugar

¼ cup sour cream

1 teaspoon vanilla extract

½ cup mashed ripe banana

2 tablespoons all-purpose flour

1 large egg

For the Topping

1 batch Caramel Dip (page 24)

2 cups thawed Cool Whip

1 firm yellow banana, sliced

Chocolate sprinkles (optional)

INSTRUCTIONS

1. Place a large rimmed baking sheet on the very bottom rack of the oven and fill it halfway with water. Preheat the oven to 350°F. Line a cupcake pan with paper liners.

2. For the Crust: Mix together the graham crackers crumbs, sugar, and melted butter. Spoon the crumbs evenly into the bottom of the paper liners. Press the crumbs down firmly. Set aside.

3. For the Cheesecake: Beat the cream cheese until creamy. Add the sugar, sour cream, and vanilla and beat until smooth.

4. Add the mashed banana and flour and mix it in thoroughly.

5. Add the egg and beat until just incorporated. Do not overbeat the batter.

6. Spoon the cheesecake batter evenly over the crusts. Place the cupcake pan on the oven rack right above the tray of water. Bake the cheesecakes for 23 to 25 minutes. They will be puffy and just slightly cracked.

(continued)

7. Remove the pan from the oven and place it on a wire rack. Let the cheesecakes cool in the pan for 10 minutes. They will flatten out as they cool.

8. Gently remove the cheesecakes from the cupcake pan and place them on the wire rack. Let the cheesecakes cool for 1 hour, then refrigerate them for 2 to 3 hours, or until completely chilled.

9. <u>For the Topping:</u> Right before serving, place a spoonful of room-temperature caramel dip onto the top of each cheesecake cupcake.

10. Swirl the Cool Whip on top of the caramel using a piping bag and icing tip 1M. Top each cheesecake with a fresh banana slice and chocolate sprinkles right before serving.

Skinny Mini Cheesecakes

PREP TIME: 20 MINUTES | **BAKE TIME:** 22 MINUTES | **SERVING:** MAKES 12 MINI CHEESECAKES

Just like everyone else, I go through phases of eating healthy and of eating all the things I want. As summer starts to get closer, I tend to make smarter eating choices. These little cheesecakes are made with a reduced fat cream cheese, Greek yogurt, and a little bit of honey, and they are a perfect light and sweet treat. Fresh fruit and a drizzle of honey on top give them a little bit of a sweeter taste, if you like. Eating a few of these little treats will still keep you on track for those cute summer clothes.

INGREDIENTS

1 (8-ounce) package reduced-fat cream cheese, at room temperature

¼ cup honey, plus more for drizzling

1 cup plain Greek yogurt

1 teaspoon vanilla extract

1 tablespoon lime juice

2 large egg whites

Fresh fruit, for serving

INSTRUCTIONS

1. Place a large rimmed baking sheet on the very bottom rack of the oven and fill it halfway with water. Preheat the oven to 350°F. Line a cupcake pan with foil liners.

2. Beat the cream cheese until creamy. Add the honey and beat until smooth.

3. Add the yogurt, vanilla, and lime juice and beat again.

4. Add the egg whites one at a time, beating well after each addition. Make sure the egg whites are fully incorporated, but do not overbeat the batter.

5. Divide the cheesecake batter evenly among the cupcake liners. Place the pan on the oven rack right above the tray of water. Bake for 22 to 24 minutes, or until the cheesecakes are puffy and slightly cracked.

6. Remove the pan from the oven and place it on a wire rack. Let the cheesecakes cool in the pan for 15 minutes. Gently remove the cheesecakes and place them on the wire rack.

7. Let the cheesecakes cool for 1 hour, then refrigerate them for 2 to 3 hours, or until completely chilled.

8. Serve with fresh fruit and a drizzle of honey, if desired.

Chocolate Cookies-and-Cream Cheesecakes

PREP TIME: 30 MINUTES | BAKE TIME: 22 MINUTES | SERVING: MAKES 20 MINI CHEESECAKES

If it has cookies and cream in it, our daughter will devour it. It is one of her top flavor combos. Any time I ask her opinion on what kind of cookie, pie, or cake I should make, she will reply, "Cookies and cream." So of course she requested mini cookies-and-cream cheesecakes to be added to this book. How could I say no? After all, these fun cupcakes have a layer of chocolate and then a cookies and cream mousse topping with a cute mini cookie on top! My daughter always wants me to make these for her, so I know you will love them, too.

INGREDIENTS

For the Crust

8 Oreo cookies

2 tablespoons unsalted butter, melted

For the Cheesecake

2 (8-ounce) packages cream cheese, at room temperature

½ cup sugar

¼ cup sour cream

1 teaspoon vanilla extract

4 ounces bittersweet baking chocolate, melted

2 large eggs

For the Mousse

1 (8-ounce) package cream cheese, at room temperature

¼ cup sugar

1 teaspoon vanilla extract

1 (8-ounce) container Cool Whip, thawed

7 Oreo cookies

20 mini Oreo cookies

INSTRUCTIONS

1. Place a large rimmed baking sheet on the very bottom rack of the oven and fill it halfway with water. Preheat the oven to 350°F. Line a cupcake pan with paper liners. Line 8 wells of a second cupcake pan with paper liners.

2. For the Crust: Place the cookies, cream filling included, in a food processor. Pulse until the cookies are crumbs.

3. Mix together the cookie crumbs and butter. Spoon the crumbs evenly into the cupcake liners. Press the crumbs down firmly. Set the pan aside.

4. For the Cheesecake: Beat the cream cheese until creamy. Add the sugar and beat again until smooth.

5. Add the sour cream and vanilla and beat again.

6. Add the melted chocolate into the batter and beat until incorporated.

7. Add the eggs one at a time, beating well after each addition. Make sure the eggs are fully incorporated, but do not overbeat the batter.

8.   Spoon the cheesecake batter evenly over the crusts. Place the pan on the oven rack right above the tray of water. Bake the cheesecakes for 20 to 22 minutes.

9.   Remove the pan from the oven and place it on a wire rack. Let the cheesecakes cool in the pan for 10 minutes.

10. Gently remove the cheesecakes from the pan and place them on the wire rack. Let the cheesecakes cool for 1 hour, then refrigerate them for 2 to 3 hours, or until completely chilled.

11. **For the Mousse:** Beat the cream cheese until creamy. Add the sugar and vanilla and beat until smooth.

12. Pulse the regular-size cookies, cream filling included, in a food processor until they are crumbs.

13. Gently fold the Cool Whip into the cream cheese mixture using a rubber spatula. Stir in the cookie crumbs gently.

14. Swirl the cheesecake mousse onto the tops of the chilled cupcakes using a piping bag and icing tip 1M. Top each cheesecake with a mini Oreo cookie.

Triple Peanut Butter Cheesecakes

PREP TIME: 20 MINUTES | BAKE TIME: 25 MINUTES | SERVING: MAKES 18 MINI CHEESECAKES

One of my all-time favorite candies is a Reese's peanut butter cup. When our kids were younger, they were so sweet about sharing these candies with me when they would get them from church or school. Over the years, all three of them have developed the same love for those peanut butter cups. Now they pretend they are going to share one with me, but when I reach for it, they eat it quickly. I guess that is a good thing, because those candies are just too dangerous for me to be around. One bite, and it's all over for healthy eating. Eating one candy leads to nine more candy wrappers beside me. The same thing happened with these cheesecake cupcakes. I had to keep eating them to find the hidden candy in the bottom. Yes, you heard me right. The magic of this cheesecake is that there is a special peanut butter cup surprise at the bottom of each cheesecake!

INGREDIENTS

18 full-size peanut butter cups, wrappers removed

For the Cheesecake
2 (8-ounce) packages cream cheese, at room temperature

½ cup sugar

¼ cup honey

2 tablespoons sour cream

½ cup creamy peanut butter

2 large eggs

For the Topping
¼ cup heavy cream

½ cup milk chocolate chips

1 (8-ounce) container Cool Whip, thawed

18 small peanut butter cups

Chocolate sprinkles

INSTRUCTIONS

1. Place a large rimmed baking sheet on the very bottom rack of the oven and fill it halfway with water. Preheat the oven to 350°F. Line a cupcake pan with paper liners. Line 6 wells of a second cupcake pan with paper liners.

2. Place a peanut butter cup in each paper liner. Set aside.

3. For the Cheesecake: Beat the cream cheese until creamy. Add the sugar and honey and beat until smooth.

4. Add the sour cream and peanut butter and beat until everything is incorporated.

5. Add the eggs one at a time, beating well after each addition. Make sure the eggs are fully incorporated, but do not overbeat the batter.

6. Spoon the cheesecake batter evenly into the cupcake liners. Place the pan on the oven rack right above the tray of water. Bake the cheesecakes for 25 minutes.

(continued)

7. Remove the pan from the oven and place it on a wire rack. Let the cheesecakes cool in the pan for 10 minutes. Gently remove the cheese-cakes from the pan and place them on the wire rack. Let the cheesecakes cool for 1 hour, then refrigerate them for 2 to 3 hours or until completely chilled.

8. **<u>For the Topping:</u>** Place the cream and chocolate chips in a microwave-safe bowl. Microwave for 15 to 20 seconds. Stir the chocolate until melted and creamy. Heat for 10 more seconds, if needed.

9. Spoon the chocolate evenly on top of the chilled cheesecakes. Let the chocolate set.

10. Swirl the Cool Whip on top of the chocolate with a piping bag and icing tip 1M. Top each one with a small peanut butter cup and sprinkles.

Espresso Cheesecakes

PREP TIME: 25 MINUTES | BAKE TIME: 25 MINUTES | SERVING: MAKES 12 MINI CHEESECAKES

Coffee was a drink that I learned to enjoy in college. One of my good friends would always drink a cup of coffee at breakfast, so one day I decided that I was going to start liking coffee, too. In those days, it was more cream and sugar than coffee, but it didn't matter because I felt like a "cool kid" drinking coffee each morning. I still enjoy my daily coffee, but I have learned to love it with less sugar. Just don't ask me to give up my flavored creamers! These little cheesecakes taste just like a Frappuccino from your local coffee shop. The espresso whipped cream and hot fudge drizzle add a fun little flair to the top. Pair them with a nice hot cup of coffee, and you will be all charged up for the day.

INGREDIENTS

For the Crust

10 Oreo cookies

2 tablespoons unsalted butter, melted

For the Cheesecake

1 tablespoon instant espresso powder

1 tablespoon hot water

2 (8-ounce) packages cream cheese, at room temperature

½ cup sugar

¼ cup sour cream

2 tablespoons all-purpose flour

2 large eggs

For the Topping

1 batch Espresso Whipped Cream (page 29)

¼ cup hot fudge topping

12 chocolate-covered coffee beans

INSTRUCTIONS

1. Place a large rimmed baking sheet on the very bottom rack of the oven and fill it halfway with water. Preheat the oven to 350°F. Line a cupcake pan with paper liners.

2. **For the Crust:** Place the cookies, cream filling included, in a food processor. Pulse until the cookies become crumbs.

3. Mix together the chocolate cookie crumbs and melted butter. Divide the mixture evenly among the cupcake liners. Press the crumbs down firmly. Set aside.

4. **For the Cheesecake:** Mix together the espresso powder and hot water and stir until dissolved.

5. Beat the cream cheese until creamy. Add the sugar and sour cream and beat until smooth.

6. Add the dissolved espresso and flour and beat until incorporated.

7. Add the eggs one at a time, beating well after each one. Make sure the eggs are fully incorporated, but do not overbeat the mixture.

(continued)

Espresso Cheesecakes (continued)

8. Spoon the cheesecake batter into the prepared cupcake liners. Place the cupcake pan on the oven rack right above the tray of water.

9. Bake the cheesecakes for 25 minutes. Remove the pan from the oven and place it on a wire rack. Let the cheesecakes cool in the pan for 10 minutes.

10. Gently remove the cheesecakes from the pan and place them on the wire rack. Let the cheesecakes cool for 1 hour, then refrigerate them for 2 to 3 hours, or until completely chilled.

11. **For the Topping:** Swirl the espresso whipped cream on top of the chilled cheesecakes using a piping bag and icing tip 1M.

12. Place the hot fudge in a microwave-safe bowl and microwave for 15 to 20 seconds. Stir until creamy. Drizzle the hot fudge over the tops of the cheesecakes. Top each cheesecake with a chocolate-covered coffee bean.

Nutella Mousse Cheesecakes

PREP TIME: 40 MINUTES | BAKE TIME: 18 TO 20 MINUTES | SERVING: MAKES 24 MINI CHEESECAKES

One of my guilty pleasures is eating Nutella straight from the jar with a spoon. Is there any other way to eat it, really? No one else in my house really likes that chocolate goodness, so the little jar and I hide in the pantry together from time to time to "talk." I enjoy the creamy hazelnut spread so much that I just had to make some mini cheesecakes out of it. These little cheesecakes have two times the Nutella love inside them. A layer of chocolate cheesecake, chocolate mousse, and fresh strawberries on top made these cheesecakes look absolutely gorgeous and taste even better! I almost didn't want to eat them…almost.

INGREDIENTS

For the Crust
20 Oreo cookies

4 tablespoons (½ stick) unsalted butter, melted

For the Cheesecake
2 (8-ounce) packages cream cheese, at room temperature

½ cup sugar

¼ cup sour cream

¾ cup Nutella spread

2 tablespoons unsweetened dark cocoa powder

2 large eggs

For the Mousse
1 (8-ounce) package cream cheese, at room temperature

½ cup Nutella spread

1 (12-ounce) container Cool Whip, thawed

24 fresh strawberries

INSTRUCTIONS

1. Place a large rimmed baking sheet on the very bottom rack of the oven and fill it halfway with water. Preheat the oven to 350°F. Line two cupcake pans with paper liners.

2. For the Crust: Place the cookies, cream filling included, in a food processor. Pulse until the cookies are crumbs.

3. Mix together the cookie crumbs and butter. Divide the mixture evenly among the paper liners. Press the crumbs down firmly and set aside.

4. For the Cheesecake: Beat the cream cheese until creamy. Add the sugar and sour cream and beat until smooth.

5. Add the Nutella and cocoa powder and beat until incorporated.

6. Add the eggs one at a time, beating well after each addition. Make sure the eggs are fully incorporated, but do not overbeat the batter.

7. Spoon the cheesecake batter evenly into the cupcake liners. Place the pan on the rack right above the tray of water. Bake for 18 to 20 minutes.

8. Remove the pan from the oven and place it on a wire rack. Let the cheesecakes cool in the pan for 10 minutes. Gently remove the cheesecakes from the pan and set them on the wire rack.

9. Let the cheesecakes cool for 1 hour, then refrigerate them for 2 to 3 hours, or until completely chilled.

10. <u>For the Mousse:</u> Beat the cream cheese until creamy. Add the Nutella and beat again until smooth.

11. Fold in 2 cups of the Cool Whip gently with a rubber spatula. Spoon the mixture onto the tops of the chilled cupcakes, filling the liners to the top and smoothing them flat.

12. Swirl the remaining Cool Whip on top of the cheesecakes with a piping bag and icing tip 1M. Place a fresh strawberry on top of each cheesecake right before serving.

Black Cherry–Ricotta Cheesecakes

PREP TIME: 30 MINUTES | BAKE TIME: 28 MINUTES | SERVING: MAKES 14 MINI CHEESECAKES

My husband and I love going out for lunch dates when the kids are in school. One day, we stopped at a local grocery store and restaurant. Of course, I had to scope out all the treats, because as a dessert blogger, I'm always looking for new ideas. In one of their refrigerated dessert cases, I found mini black cherry ricotta cheesecakes and had to buy one for "research purposes." It turns out that I absolutely love the flavor of ricotta cheese in a cheesecake, so I couldn't wait to re-create this delicious dessert in our kitchen. For these little cheesecakes, I made a homemade cherry filling that is swirled on top. Always be willing to be adventurous and try new things when you are out for dinner. You may just find that you like those new things and will be glad you tried them.

INGREDIENTS

For the Crust

1 cup chocolate graham cracker crumbs

1 tablespoon sugar

4 tablespoons (½ stick) unsalted butter, melted

For the Cheesecake

1 (8-ounce) package cream cheese, at room temperature

1 cup ricotta cheese, drained if needed

½ cup sugar

¼ cup heavy cream

2 teaspoons vanilla extract

2 tablespoons all-purpose flour

2 large eggs

1 batch Fruit Filling (page 26; use 2 cups quartered frozen black cherries)

INSTRUCTIONS

1. Place a large rimmed baking sheet on the very bottom rack of the oven and fill it halfway with water. Preheat the oven to 350°F. Line a cupcake pan with paper liners. Line two wells of a second cupcake pan with paper liners.

2. For the Crust: Mix together the graham cracker crumbs, sugar, and melted butter. Spoon the mixture evenly into the cupcake liners. Press the crumbs down firmly. Set aside.

3. For the Cheesecake: Beat the cream cheese until creamy. Add the ricotta cheese and sugar and beat until smooth.

4. Add the cream, vanilla, and flour and beat until incorporated.

5. Add the eggs one at a time, beating well after each addition. Make sure the eggs are fully incorporated, but do not overbeat the mixture.

6. Spoon the cheesecake batter into the prepared cupcake liners. Top each cupcake with a tablespoon of the cherry filling. Use a butter knife to gently swirl the cheesecake and filling together.

7. Place the pan on the oven rack right above the tray of water. Bake for 28 minutes, or until the cheesecakes are puffy and slightly cracked. Remove the pan from the oven and place it on a wire rack. Let the cheesecakes cool in the pan for 10 minutes. They will flatten as they cool.

8. Gently remove the cheesecakes from the pan and place them on the wire rack. Let the cheesecakes cool for 1 hour, then refrigerate them for 2 to 3 hours or until completely chilled.

Note. You can use your favorite frozen fruit in place of the cherries, if desired.

Pumpkin Oreo Cheesecakes

PREP TIME: 25 MINUTES | **BAKE TIME:** 25 MINUTES | **SERVING:** MAKES 18 MINI CHEESECAKES

I really do try to wait until October to break out the pumpkin in our kitchen, but usually I get so anxious and excited for pumpkin season that I open a can or two in September. Okay, fine, I have been known to bake with pumpkin a few times in August, too. Pumpkin lovers will get that! These fun treats were one of the first cheesecakes I shared on the blog quite a few years ago during the fall pumpkin season. I was playing around with a fun and different way to do a pumpkin dessert, and now they are always very popular with my readers around the holidays. The cookie layers on the bottom and the top give it such a fun little twist that everyone loves.

INGREDIENTS

For the Crust

18 Oreo cookies

For the Cheesecake

2 (8-ounce) packages cream cheese, at room temperature

½ cup sugar

2 tablespoons sour cream

1 cup canned pumpkin puree

1 teaspoon vanilla extract

1 teaspoon ground cinnamon

½ teaspoon ground nutmeg

2 tablespoons all-purpose flour

2 large eggs

For the Topping

1 (8-ounce) container Cool Whip, thawed

4 Oreo cookies

INSTRUCTIONS

1. Place a large rimmed baking sheet on the very bottom rack of the oven and fill it halfway with water. Preheat the oven to 350°F. Line a cupcake pan with paper liners. Line six wells of a second cupcake pan with paper liners.

2. **For the Crust:** Take the Oreo cookies and split them apart. Place one cookie half, cream filling–side up, into the bottom of each cupcake liner. Set aside, reserving the remaining cookie halves.

3. **For the Cheesecake:** Beat the cream cheese until creamy. Add the sugar, sour cream, pumpkin, and vanilla and beat until smooth.

4. Add the cinnamon, nutmeg, and flour and beat until incorporated.

5. Add the eggs one at a time, beating well after each addition. Make sure the eggs are fully incorporated, but do not overbeat the mixture.

(continued)

6. Spoon the cheesecake batter evenly and carefully into the prepared cupcake liners. Place the remaining cookie halves on top of the cheesecake batter, cream filling–side down.

7. Place the cupcake pan on the rack right above the tray of water. Bake the cheesecakes for 25 minutes. Remove the pan from the oven and place it on a wire rack. Let the cheesecakes cool in the pan for 10 minutes.

8. Gently remove the cheesecakes from the pan and place them on the wire rack. Let the cheesecakes cool for 1 hour, then refrigerate them for 2 to 3 hours, or until completely chilled.

9. <u>**For the Topping:**</u> Swirl the Cool Whip on top of the chilled cheesecake using a piping bag and icing tip 1M.

10. Break three of the cookies into 18 small chunks. Place the cookie chunks on top of each cheesecake. Crush the remaining cookie into fine crumbs and sprinkle on top of each cheesecake.

White Chocolate Mint Cheesecakes

PREP TIME: 25 MINUTES | BAKE TIME: 25 MINUTES | SERVING: MAKES 18 MINI CHEESECAKES

Pairing chocolate and mint around the holidays seems like a natural thing to do. These fun little cheesecakes have a pretty green swirl of mint on top of a creamy white chocolate cheesecake. Adding a chocolate mint cookie crust just adds to the flavor explosion in your mouth. Bring them to all those family and work parties and watch the cheesecakes disappear right before your eyes. But unless you want coal in your stocking, you might want to save a couple for Santa and his reindeer!

INGREDIENTS

For the Crust

35 Grasshopper cookies

4 tablespoons (½ stick) unsalted butter, melted

For the Cheesecake

2 (8-ounce) packages cream cheese, at room temperature

½ cup sugar

2 tablespoons sour cream

2 tablespoons all-purpose flour

4 ounces white baking chocolate, melted

2 large eggs

For the Mint Mousse

1 (8-ounce) package cream cheese, at room temperature

2 ounces white baking chocolate, melted

2 cups Cool Whip, thawed

¾ teaspoon mint extract

Green gel color

¼ cup mint baking chips

INSTRUCTIONS

1. Place a large rimmed baking sheet on the very bottom rack of the oven and fill it halfway with water. Preheat the oven to 350°F. Line a cupcake pan with paper liners. Line six wells of a second cupcake pan with paper liners.

2. **For the Crust:** Place the cookies in a food processor and pulse until the cookies become crumbs.

3. Mix together the cookie crumbs and melted butter. Spoon the mixture evenly into the cupcake liners. Press the crumbs down firmly. Set aside.

4. **For the Cheesecake:** Beat the cream cheese until creamy. Add the sugar and sour cream and beat until smooth. Stir in the flour.

5. Add the melted chocolate and beat until completely incorporated.

6. Add the eggs one at a time, beating well after each addition. Make sure the eggs are fully incorporated, but do not overbeat the batter.

(continued)

7. Spoon the cheesecake batter into the prepared cupcake liners. Place the pan on the oven rack right above the tray of water. Bake the cheesecakes for 25 minutes.

8. Remove the pan from the oven and place it on a wire rack. Let the cheesecakes cool in the pan for 10 minutes.

9. Gently remove the cheesecakes from the pan and place them on the wire rack. Let the cheesecakes cool for 1 hour, then refrigerate them for 2 to 3 hours, or until completely chilled.

10. <u>For the Mint Mousse:</u> Beat the cream cheese until creamy. Add the melted chocolate and beat until smooth.

11. Use a rubber spatula to fold in the Cool Whip gently until completely incorporated. Gently stir in the mint extract.

12. Use a toothpick to add a little bit of green gel color to the mixture. Stir the color in. Continue to add more green with a clean toothpick until you get the color you want. Keep in mind that the color will deepen the longer it sits.

13. Swirl the mint mousse on the tops of the cheesecakes using a piping bag and icing tip 1M. Sprinkle the tops of the cheesecakes with the mint baking chips.

3

Cheesecake Bars & Bites

×

DOUBLE TROUBLE

I just *cannot* choose my favorite dessert, so most of the time I end up combining a few of my favorites into one glorious treat. And let me tell you, there is something so comforting about biting into a cookie bar that has a ribbon of cheesecake running through it. Pop a few of those in your freezer for the next time your sweet tooth needs to be satisfied!

Chocolate Chip Cheesecake Bars

PREP TIME: 30 MINUTES | **BAKE TIME:** 45 MINUTES | **SERVING:** MAKES 24 BARS

Chocolate Chip Cheesecake Bars! Say that five times fast…Okay, forget about saying it—eating five of them is easier. A chocolate cookie crust topped with creamy cheesecake creates a delicious treat to make and share at picnics and parties. Who doesn't love a dessert loaded with lots of chocolate chips? Not this girl! I tend to buy my chocolate chips by the case and then load them into my scrumptious desserts. So open a bag of chocolate chips, and let's get after it!

INGREDIENTS

For the Crust

30 Oreo cookies

6 tablespoons (¾ stick) unsalted butter, melted

For the Cheesecake

3 (8-ounce) packages cream cheese, at room temperature

1½ cups sugar

¼ cup sour cream

2 teaspoons vanilla extract

¼ cup all-purpose flour

3 large eggs

1¼ cups mini chocolate chips

INSTRUCTIONS

1. Preheat the oven to 325°F. Line a 9 x 13-inch baking pan with aluminum foil and spray it with nonstick baking spray.

2. **For the Crust:** Place the cookies, cream filling included, in a food processor. Pulse the cookies until they become crumbs.

3. Mix together the cookie crumbs and melted butter. Press the mixture evenly into the bottom of the prepared pan. Bake the crust for 10 minutes. Remove the pan from the oven and let the crust cool for at least 20 minutes. Keep the oven on.

4. Place a large rimmed baking sheet on the very bottom rack of the oven and fill it halfway with water.

5. **For the Cheesecake:** Beat the cream cheese until creamy. Add the sugar, sour cream, and vanilla and beat until smooth.

6. Add the flour and beat again.

(continued)

7. Add the eggs one at a time, beating well after each addition. Make sure the eggs are fully incorporated, but do not overbeat the batter. Stir in 1 cup of the mini chocolate chips by hand.

8. Pour the cheesecake batter over the cooled crust. Sprinkle the top of the cheesecake with the remaining mini chocolate chips. Place the pan on the oven rack right above the tray of water. Bake the cheesecake for 45 minutes.

9. Remove the pan from the oven and place it on a wire rack. Let the cheesecake cool for 1 hour, and then refrigerate it for 4 hours or until completely chilled. Cut the cheesecake into 24 bars before serving.

Snickerdoodle Cheesecake Cookie Bars

PREP TIME: 25 MINUTES | BAKE TIME: 30 MINUTES | SERVING: MAKES 24 BARS

Cheesecake cookie bars were one of the very first recipes that I shared on the blog years ago. It makes me laugh every time I see the bad pictures I took of them, but I leave those pictures there as a reminder of how much I have learned over the years. Another thing I have learned since then is to make homemade cookie dough. Now, sometimes using a roll of the refrigerated cookie dough is necessary. Believe me, I still do it from time to time. For these homemade cookie bars, I changed up the dough and added quite a bit of cinnamon and nutmeg to get that sweet snickerdoodle taste. As we were testing all these recipes, my husband's job was to get the sweets out of the house. Boy, was I glad he took these to work, because I seriously couldn't stop taking pieces out of the pan.

INGREDIENTS

For the Cookies

1 cup (2 sticks) unsalted butter, at room temperature

½ cup granulated sugar

1½ cups packed brown sugar

2 large eggs

2 teaspoons vanilla extract

1 teaspoon cream of tartar

1 teaspoon baking powder

½ teaspoon salt

1 teaspoon ground cinnamon

½ teaspoon ground nutmeg

2¾ cups all-purpose flour

For the Cheesecake

1 (8-ounce) package cream cheese, at room temperature

½ cup granulated sugar

1 teaspoon vanilla extract

1 large egg

INSTRUCTIONS

1. Preheat the oven to 350°F. Line a 9 x 13-inch baking pan with aluminum foil and spray it with nonstick baking spray.

2. **For the Cookies:** Beat the butter and sugars until creamy and fluffy. Add the eggs and vanilla and beat again.

3. Stir together the cream of tartar, baking powder, salt, cinnamon, nutmeg, and flour in a bowl. Slowly add the dry ingredients to the butter mixture and beat until a soft dough forms. Divide the dough in half.

4. Press half the cookie dough evenly into the bottom of the prepared pan. Set the other half of the cookie dough aside.

5. **For the Cheesecake:** Beat the cream cheese until creamy. Add the granulated sugar and vanilla and beat until smooth.

(continued)

Snickerdoodle Cheesecake Cookie Bars (continued)

For the Topping

3 tablespoons granulated sugar

2 teaspoons ground cinnamon

6. Add the egg and beat it until fully incorporated. Do not overbeat the batter. Pour the cheesecake on top of the cookie dough in the baking dish.

7. Crumble the remaining cookie dough over the top of the cheesecake layer.

8. **For the Topping:** Stir together the granulated sugar and cinnamon and sprinkle over the top of the cheesecake and cookie dough.

9. Bake the cheesecake for 30 minutes. Remove the pan from the oven and place it on a wire rack.

10. Let the cheesecake cool for 1 hour, then refrigerate for 2 to 3 hours, or until completely chilled. Cut the cheesecake into 24 bars before serving.

Piña Colada Cheesecake Cookie Cups

PREP TIME: 30 MINUTES | BAKE TIME: 11 TO 12 MINUTES | SERVING: MAKES 24 COOKIES

Our family loves to travel for our vacations. Most of those vacations usually involve a beach at some point. The three kids head right for the water when we get there, and my husband and I relax in beach chairs with a fruity drink in hand while we watch them. I love the combo of coconut and pineapple together, so I wanted to re-create that fun beach drink in a little handheld cheesecake treat. I already have requests for more of these cookies cups from friends at church, so I think they were a huge success with everyone we shared them with, too. So if you can't make it to the beach as often as you would like, maybe one of this cookie cups will "tide" you over.

INGREDIENTS

For the Cookies

1 batch Cookie Dough (page 31)

1½ teaspoons coconut extract

½ teaspoon rum extract

1 cup sweetened shredded coconut

For the Cheesecake

1 (8-ounce) package cream cheese, at room temperature

¼ cup sugar

¾ cup crushed pineapple, drained very well

1 (8-ounce) container Cool Whip, thawed

For the Topping

24 maraschino cherries with the stems, drained and patted dry

½ cup Toasted Coconut (page 30)

INSTRUCTIONS

1. Preheat the oven to 375°F. Spray two mini-tart pans with nonstick baking spray.

2. For the Cookies: Make the cookie dough using the coconut and rum extracts in place of the vanilla extract. Gently stir the shredded coconut into the dough.

3. Roll the dough into 24 even balls. Place each dough ball into a well of the prepared tart pan. Bake the cookies for 11 to 12 minutes.

4. Remove the pan from the oven and let the cookies cool in the pan for 2 minutes.

5. Use a tart shaper (see Note) to press in the centers of the cookies. Let them cool for 2 to 3 minutes in the pan, then gently transfer the cookies to a wire rack to cool completely.

6. For the Cheesecake Filling: Beat the cream cheese until creamy. Add the sugar and beat until smooth.

(continued)

7. Stir in the drained pineapple, then fold in the Cool Whip with a rubber spatula. Spoon the cheesecake mixture evenly into the cooled cookies.

8. <u>For the Topping:</u> Top each cookie with a maraschino cherry and sprinkle the toasted coconut around the edges of the cheesecake filling.

Note. A tart shaper is a wooden tool that presses pastry and dough down into cavities of pans.

Salted Caramel Fudge Cheesecake Bars

PREP TIME: 25 MINUTES | **BAKE TIME:** 45 MINUTES | **SERVING:** MAKES 24 BARS

I love cheesecakes that have a fun swirl on top of them. Okay, I love all cheesecake, but swirls add a cool twist. These swirls look intricate, but they are actually so easy to do. After you spread the batter in the pan, you drop the fudge in randomly. A butter knife is the only tool you need to create a fun swirl pattern. Drag the knife through the batter, going up and down and side to side. Just be careful that you do not have too much fun swirling because it can go from pretty swirl to ugly swirl in a matter of seconds. The fun part about these bars is that no two pans will be identical. So just have fun with it!

INGREDIENTS

For the Crust

3 cups shortbread cookie crumbs

6 tablespoons (¾ stick) unsalted butter, melted

For the Cheesecake

3 (8-ounce) packages cream cheese, at room temperature

1 cup packed brown sugar

¼ cup sour cream

½ cup Salted Caramel Topping (page 25)

¼ cup all-purpose flour

3 large eggs

¼ cup hot fudge topping

Coarse sea salt (optional)

INSTRUCTIONS

1. Place a large rimmed baking sheet on the very bottom rack of the oven and fill it halfway with water. Preheat the oven to 325°F. Line a 9 x 13-inch baking dish with foil and spray it with nonstick spray.

2. <u>For the Crust:</u> Mix together the shortbread crumbs and melted butter. Press the mixture firmly into the bottom of the prepared pan. Set the pan aside.

3. <u>For the Cheesecake:</u> Beat the cream cheese until creamy. Add the brown sugar, sour cream, and caramel topping and beat until smooth. Stir in the flour until incorporated.

4. Add the eggs one at a time, beating well after each addition. Make sure the eggs are fully incorporated, but do not overbeat the cheesecake batter.

5. Place ¼ cup of the batter in a bowl and set aside. Pour the remaining cheesecake batter over the crust.

(continued)

6. Place the hot fudge in a microwave-safe bowl and microwave for 15 to 20 seconds, or until melted and creamy but not too hot. Stir the reserved cheesecake batter into the hot fudge.

7. Place small amounts of the hot fudge mixture randomly over the top of the batter in the pan. Gently use a butter knife to swirl the batters together. Do not let the knife go all the way down to the crust.

8. Place the pan on the oven rack right above the tray of water. Bake the cheesecake for 45 to 50 minutes.

9. Remove the cheesecake from the oven and place it on a wire rack. Let the cheesecake cool for 1 hour, then refrigerate it for 2 to 3 hours, or until completely chilled.

10. Cut into 24 bars. Sprinkle with sea salt immediately before serving, if desired.

Chocolate-Dipped Key Lime Cheesecake Squares

PREP TIME: 2 HOURS | **BAKE TIME:** 48 TO 50 MINUTES | **SERVINGS:** MAKES 72 SMALL SQUARES OR 24 REGULAR-SIZE BARS

After getting married, we celebrated our honeymoon in Key West. Since we were just out of college, we were on a very tight budget. Most days we walked from our hotel to the beach or wherever else we wanted to explore. One day, we splurged and rented a scooter so that we could see more of the island. While exploring, we found a little pie shop that sold frozen key lime pie on a stick. You could either get it plain or covered in chocolate. You know which one I chose, right? Chocolate all the way, baby! These little cheesecake squares on a stick remind me so much of our honeymoon days! One bite, and I'm instantly transported back to the island without a care in the world.

INGREDIENTS

For the Crust
1½ cups graham cracker crumbs

6 tablespoons (3/4 stick) unsalted butter, melted

For the Cheesecake
3 (8-ounce) packages cream cheese, at room temperature

1½ cups sugar

¾ cup key lime juice

6 tablespoons all-purpose flour

3 large eggs

For the Coating
4½ cups chocolate melting wafers

1 cup white chocolate melting wafers

Green sprinkles (optional)

INSTRUCTIONS

1. Place a large rimmed baking sheet on the very bottom rack of the oven and fill it with water. Preheat the oven to 325°F. Line a 9 x 13-inch baking pan with aluminum foil and spray it with nonstick baking spray.

2. For the Crust: Mix together the graham cracker crumbs and melted butter. Press the mixture firmly into the bottom of the prepared pan. Set the pan aside.

3. For the Cheesecake: Beat the cream cheese until creamy. Add the sugar and lime juice and beat until smooth. Stir in the flour until incorporated.

4. Add the eggs one at a time, beating well after each addition. Make sure the eggs are fully incorporated, but do not overbeat the batter.

5. Pour the cheesecake batter over the prepared crust. Place the pan on the oven rack right above the tray of water. Bake the cheesecake for 48 to 50 minutes.

6. Remove the pan from the oven and place it on a wire rack.

7. Let the cheesecake cool for 1 hour, then refrigerate it for 3 to 4 hours, or until completely chilled.

8. Line a baking sheet with wax paper. Lift the cheesecake out of the pan. Remove the foil from the bottom. Cut the cheesecake into seventy-two 1-inch squares. Place a small wooden Popsicle stick into the top of each one, but do not go all the way to the crust. Place the squares on the prepared baking sheet and freeze for at least 1 hour.

9. **For the Coating:** Melt the chocolate melting wafers according to the package directions. Dip the cheesecake squares into the chocolate one at a time. Use a spoon to cover the squares completely with chocolate, if necessary. Carefully tap the side of the bowl with the Popsicle stick to remove excess chocolate. Return the chocolate-covered square to the wax paper–lined baking sheet to set up. Reheat the chocolate as needed until all the squares have been dipped.

10. Melt the white chocolate wafers according to the package directions. Drizzle the white chocolate over the tops of the dipped cheesecake squares. Top with sprinkles, if desired.

Optional: Cut the cheesecake into 24 bars. Melt 1 cup chocolate melting wafers. Drizzle the melted chocolate over the tops of the cut bars instead of covering them completely in chocolate.

Turtle Cheesecake Cookie Bars

PREP TIME: 45 MINUTES | **BAKE TIME:** 28 TO 30 MINUTES | **SERVING:** MAKES 24 BARS

What do you get when you combine chocolate cookies and nuts with a caramel cheesecake? A fun twist to the turtle candies that everyone makes at the holidays, that's what! I loaded these cheesecake cookie bars with plenty of that gooey turtle goodness. I dare you to eat only one!

INGREDIENTS

For the Cookies

½ cup (1 stick) unsalted butter, at room temperature

½ cup vegetable shortening

½ cup granulated sugar

1 cup packed brown sugar

2 large eggs

1 teaspoon vanilla extract

1 tablespoon cornstarch

½ teaspoon baking soda

½ teaspoon salt

2½ cups all-purpose flour

½ cup unsweetened dark cocoa powder

For the Cheesecake

1 (8-ounce) package cream cheese, at room temperature

½ cup packed brown sugar

¼ cup Caramel Topping (page 25)

2 tablespoons all-purpose flour

1 large egg

INSTRUCTIONS

1. Preheat the oven to 350°F. Line a 9 x 13-inch baking pan with aluminum foil and spray it with nonstick baking spray.

2. **For the Cookies:** Beat the butter, shortening, and sugars until light and fluffy. Add the eggs and vanilla and beat until creamy.

3. Stir together the cornstarch, baking soda, salt, flour, and cocoa powder in a bowl. Slowly add the dry ingredients to the butter mixture and beat until a soft dough forms.

4. Press half the cookie dough into the bottom of the prepared pan. Set the pan aside. Reserve the remaining cookie dough.

5. **For the Cheesecake:** Beat the cream cheese until creamy. Add the brown sugar and beat until smooth.

6. Add the caramel and flour and beat until creamy.

7. Add the egg and beat gently until completely incorporated. Do not overbeat the batter. Pour the cheesecake batter over the cookie dough in the pan.

8. Crumble the remaining cookie dough on top of the cheesecake.

9. Bake for 28 to 30 minutes.

For the Topping

1 cup dark chocolate chips

¾ cup heavy cream

18 caramel candies, unwrapped

¼ cup finely chopped pecans

10. Remove the pan from the oven and place it on a wire rack. Let the cheesecake cool for 1 hour, then refrigerate it for 3 to 4 hours, or until completely chilled.

11. For the Topping: Place the chocolate chips and ½ cup of the heavy cream in a microwave-safe bowl. Microwave for 15 to 20 seconds. Stir until the chocolate is melted and creamy. Heat for 15 more seconds, if needed.

12. Spread the chocolate evenly on top of the cooled cheesecake with an offset spatula. Let the chocolate set before cutting the cheesecake into 24 bars.

13. Place the caramel candies and remaining ¼ cup cream in a small saucepan. Stir over low heat until the candies are melted and creamy. Let the caramel mixture cool for 7 to 8 minutes.

14. Drizzle the caramel evenly over the tops of the cheesecake squares. Sprinkle the cheesecake squares with the chopped pecans while the caramel is still wet.

Peanut Butter & Banana Bacon Cheesecake Bars

PREP TIME: 30 MINUTES   BAKE TIME: 40 MINUTES   SERVING: MAKES 24 BARS

My love for bacon used to be limited to BLT sandwiches in the summer. There is just something about warm summer tomatoes and crispy bacon that I cannot get enough of. And it does have to be crispy bacon for me to like it. My brother and brother-in-law were convinced that I had to create a cheesecake with crispy bacon on it, so I agreed to think about it. After a few months of "thinking," I remembered my husband telling me about the Elvis sandwich, which is peanut butter, banana, and bacon. Right away I knew that this combo would make a wild and crazy cheesecake flavor. The bacon on top adds a salty crunch that pairs so well with the peanut butter and banana layers. So as Elvis would say, "Put a chain around my neck" and lead me to those cheesecake bars, because my bacon horizon just expanded to sweets.

INGREDIENTS

For the Cookie Crust

4 tablespoons (½ stick) unsalted butter, at room temperature

¼ cup vegetable shortening

¼ cup granulated sugar

½ cup packed brown sugar

½ cup creamy peanut butter

1 large egg

½ teaspoon vanilla extract

¼ teaspoon salt

¼ teaspoon baking soda

1¼ cups all-purpose flour

For the Cheesecake

2 (8-ounce) packages cream cheese, at room temperature

½ cup granulated sugar

¼ cup sour cream

INSTRUCTIONS

1. Preheat the oven to 350°F. Line a 9 x 13-inch baking pan with aluminum foil and spray it with nonstick baking spray.

2. **For the Cookie Crust:** Beat the butter, shortening, and sugars until light and fluffy. Add the peanut butter, egg, and vanilla and beat until creamy.

3. Stir together the salt, baking soda, and flour in a bowl. Slowly add the dry ingredients to the butter mixture and beat until a soft dough forms.

4. Press the cookie dough evenly into the bottom of the prepared pan. Bake the crust for 15 minutes.

5. Remove the pan from the oven and place it on a wire rack. Keep the oven on. Poke the cookie with the tip of a knife all over the top. Do not go all the way through the cookie. Let the cookie cool for at least 20 minutes.

(continued)

½ cup mashed ripe banana

1 teaspoon vanilla extract

2 tablespoons all-purpose flour

1 large egg

For the Topping

1½ cups Cool Whip, thawed

1¼ cups crumbled cooked crispy bacon

6. Place a large rimmed baking sheet on the very bottom rack of the oven and fill it halfway with water.

7. **For the Cheesecake:** Beat the cream cheese until creamy. Add the granulated sugar, sour cream, and vanilla and beat until smooth.

8. Add the banana and flour and beat until incorporated.

9. Add the egg and beat until just incorporated. Do not overbeat the batter. Spread the cheesecake batter over the cooled cookie crust.

10. Place the pan on the oven rack right above the tray of water. Bake the cheesecake for 25 minutes.

11. Remove the pan from the oven and place it on a wire rack. Let the cheesecake cool for 1 hour, then refrigerate it for 4 hours, or until completely chilled.

12. **For the Topping:** Spread the Cool Whip over the cooled cheesecake with an offset spatula. Right before serving, sprinkle the crumbled bacon over the top of the cheesecake and cut into 24 bars.

Monster Cookie Chocolate Cheesecake Bars

PREP TIME: 30 MINUTES | BAKE TIME: 35 MINUTES | SERVING: MAKES 24 BARS

Whenever we need a dessert for a picnic or party, I make cheesecake cookie bars. They are easy to put together, and if you cut them small enough, they feed a big crowd. And who doesn't love a loaded cookie bar, right? Especially a cookie bar that has peanut butter, chocolate candies, and cheesecake all baked together. If you don't want to cut them into small pieces, you can leave it uncut and have "one" cookie all to yourself!

INGREDIENTS

For the Cookie Crust

½ cup (1 stick) unsalted butter, at room temperature

½ cup granulated sugar

1 cup packed brown sugar

1 cup creamy peanut butter

2 large eggs

1 teaspoon vanilla extract

½ teaspoon salt

½ teaspoon baking soda

2 cups all-purpose flour

1 cup quick-cooking oats

2 tablespoons milk

1 cup chocolate chips

1 cup M&M's candies, divided

For the Cheesecake

2 (8-ounce) packages cream cheese, at room temperature

½ cup granulated sugar

4 ounces semisweet baking chocolate, melted

2 large eggs

INSTRUCTIONS

1. Preheat the oven to 350°F. Line a 9 x 13-inch baking pan with aluminum foil and spray it with nonstick baking spray.

2. **For the Cookie Crust:** Beat the butter and sugars until light and fluffy. Add the peanut butter and beat until creamy.

3. Add the eggs and vanilla and beat again.

4. Stir together the salt, baking soda, flour, and oats in a bowl. Slowly add the dry ingredients to the butter mixture and beat until incorporated. Add the milk and beat again.

5. Stir in the chocolate chips and ¾ cup M&M's candies by hand.

6. Press half the cookie dough into the bottom of the prepared pan. Set the pan aside. Reserve the remaining dough.

7. **For the Cheesecake:** Beat the cream cheese until creamy. Add the granulated sugar and beat until smooth.

8. Add the melted chocolate and beat until creamy.

(continued)

9. Add the eggs one at a time, beating well after each addition. Make sure the eggs are fully incorporated, but do not overbeat the batter.

10. Spread the cheesecake batter over the cookie dough in the pan. Crumble the remaining cookie dough over the cheesecake batter. Sprinkle the remaining M&M's on top.

11. Bake the cheesecake for 35 minutes.

12. Remove the pan from the oven and place it on a wire rack. Let the cheesecake cool for 1 hour, then refrigerate it for 4 hours, or until completely chilled. Cut into 24 bars before serving.

4

No-Bake Cheesecakes

⋯⋯⋯ ✕ ⋯⋯⋯

EASY-PEASY!

There is so much you can do with cheesecake and so many mind-blowing flavor combinations to try! But sometimes I just do not want to take the time to turn on the oven. For times like this, I turn to no-bake cheesecakes. Cheesecake goodness in a matter of minutes…now *that's* what I'm talkin' about. Plus, no-bake cheesecakes in jars make the cutest parties treats or favors. Think of all the possibilities for decorating those jars with ribbons and bows.

No-Bake Malt Cheesecake

PREP TIME: 30 MINUTES | **SERVING:** MAKES ONE 9-INCH CHEESECAKE (12 SLICES)

Growing up, my parents did all of our grocery shopping for the week on Friday nights. Sometimes they were brave and took all five of us kids shopping with them. We always tried to convince them to get a box of malt balls before we left the store. My favorites were the ones that just had a chewy chocolate shell. To this day I cannot eat malt balls without thinking of those shopping trips. I added malt powder and crushed malt candies to this no-bake cheesecake. Chocolate and more malt candies make the cheesecake so pretty. Gotta love a fun dessert that brings back childhood memories!

INGREDIENTS

For the Crust

1½ cups chocolate graham cracker crumbs

½ cup (1 stick) unsalted butter, melted

For the Cheesecake

2 (8-ounce) packages cream cheese, at room temperature

¾ cup powdered sugar

½ cup sour cream

1 teaspoon vanilla extract

¼ teaspoon salt

½ cup original malt powder

1 (8-ounce) container Cool Whip, thawed

1 cup coarsely crushed malt balls

For the Topping

½ cup milk chocolate chips

¼ cup heavy cream

12 whole malt ball candies

INSTRUCTIONS

1. **For the Crust:** Line a 9-inch springform pan with parchment paper. Mix together the graham cracker crumbs and butter. Press the mixture evenly into the bottom of the prepared pan. Place the pan in the refrigerator.

2. **For the Cheesecake:** Beat the cream cheese until creamy. Add the powdered sugar and sour cream and beat until smooth.

3. Add the vanilla, salt, and malt powder and beat again.

4. Use a rubber spatula to gently fold in 2 cups of the Cool Whip. Stir the crushed malt balls into the batter.

5. Spread the filling over the prepared crust. Refrigerate for at least 2 hours.

6. **For the Topping:** Place the chocolate chips and heavy cream in a microwave-safe bowl. Microwave for 20 to 30 seconds. Stir the chocolate until melted and creamy. Spread the chocolate over the chilled cheesecake using an offset spatula.

7. Swirl the remaining Cool Whip around the edges using a piping bag and icing tip 27. Top the swirls with the malt balls.

No-Bake Neapolitan Cheesecake Cups

PREP TIME: 30 MINUTES | **SERVING:** MAKES 4 LARGE PARFAITS

Chocolate, vanilla, and strawberry is a classic flavor combo that is sure to please. It is the perfect gallon of ice cream to have at birthday parties because it covers almost everyone's favorites. I wanted a no-bake jar treat that had those same fun ice cream flavors but with a no-bake cheesecake flair. These are so pretty and would be perfect for baby or bridal showers.

INGREDIENTS

For the Crust
10 Oreo cookies

For the Vanilla Cheesecake
1 (8-ounce) package cream cheese, at room temperature

2 tablespoons sugar

1 teaspoon vanilla extract

½ cup marshmallow crème

1½ cups Cool Whip, thawed

For the Strawberry Cheesecake
1 (8-ounce) package cream cheese, at room temperature

2 tablespoons sugar

1 tablespoon unflavored powdered gelatin

2 tablespoons boiling water

1 cup diced strawberries

½ cup Cool Whip, thawed

For the Topping
2 tablespoons heavy cream

¼ cup dark chocolate chips

4 fresh strawberries

INSTRUCTIONS

1. **For the Crust:** Place the cookies, cream filling included, in a food processor. Pulse until the cookies become crumbs.

2. Divide the cookie crumbs evenly among four large parfait glasses. Set the glasses aside.

3. **For the Vanilla Cheesecake:** Beat the cream cheese until creamy. Add the sugar and beat until smooth.

4. Add the vanilla and marshmallow crème and beat until creamy. Fold in the Cool Whip using a rubber spatula. Spoon the cheesecake mixture into the parfait glasses very gently. Use the back of a spoon to spread it flat.

5. **For the Strawberry Cheesecake:** Beat the cream cheese until creamy. Add the sugar and beat until smooth.

6. Dissolve the gelatin in the boiling water. Puree the strawberries in a food processor or blender. Add the dissolved gelatin and pulse briefly to combine. Add the mixture to the cream cheese and beat until smooth.

(continued)

7. Gently fold in the Cool Whip using a rubber spatula. Spoon the strawberry cheesecake onto the vanilla cheesecake layer. Use the back of a spoon to spread it flat, if needed. Place the glasses in the refrigerator and chill for at least 1 hour.

8. <u>For the Topping:</u> Place the cream and chocolate chips in a microwave-safe bowl. Microwave for 15 to 20 seconds. Stir the chocolate until melted and creamy.

9. Spoon the chocolate evenly onto the strawberry cheesecake layer. Place the glasses in the refrigerator until the chocolate is set. Place a fresh strawberry on top of each parfait immediately before serving.

Note. You could also divide the crumbs and cheesecake layers into eight small 4-ounce parfait glasses or jars.

No-Bake Salted Caramel Cheesecake Tarts

PREP TIME: 30 MINUTES | **SERVING:** 30 CHEESECAKE TARTS

I adore all things salted caramel. These little tarts start out with prepackaged pastry shells. Some days, store-bought conveniences just make life easier. A layer of creamy chocolate is hidden under a no-bake salted caramel cheesecake swirl. These little treats seriously come together in no time at all. They are a cute dessert to share with your family and friends. Plus, they look like they came from the bakery, so no one will know you put them together in less than 30 minutes in your own kitchen.

INGREDIENTS

2 (15-count) packages fully baked mini phyllo shells, thawed

For the Chocolate
½ cup dark chocolate chips
¼ cup heavy cream

For the Whipped Cream
½ cup heavy cream
2 tablespoons powdered sugar

For the Cheesecake
1 (8-ounce) package cream cheese, at room temperature
½ cup plus 1 tablespoon powdered sugar
½ cup dulce de leche
½ teaspoon coarse sea salt
30 pecan halves

INSTRUCTIONS

1. Set the phyllo shells on a rimmed baking sheet.

2. **For the Chocolate:** Place the chocolate chips and cream in a microwave-safe bowl. Microwave for 20 to 30 seconds. Stir until the chocolate is melted and creamy. Divide the chocolate mixture evenly among the phyllo shells.

3. **For the Whipped Cream:** Beat the cream and powdered sugar on high until stiff peaks form. Set aside.

4. **For the Cheesecake:** Beat the cream cheese until creamy. Add the powdered sugar and beat until smooth.

5. Add the dulce de leche and beat until creamy.

6. Gently fold in the whipped cream with a rubber spatula. Stir in the sea salt.

7. Pipe the mixture on top of the chocolate in the shells using a piping bag and 1M icing tip. Place a pecan half on top of each cheesecake swirl.

No-Bake Strawberry Cheesecake Parfaits

PREP TIME: 25 MINUTES | **SERVING:** MAKES SIX 8-OUNCE JARS

I never realized how long it took to fill a basket with berries, until I took our kids strawberry picking for the first time when they were little. They all started out picking berries like champs, but then slowly, the flowers, bugs, and juicy berries distracted them. Every time I would look over, one of them was taking a "break" and eating a few berries from the baskets. It's a good thing places like that don't weigh your kids in and out, because they would eat their fair share of berries in the field. To this day, every time I eat strawberries I think about being in the fields under the warm sun, picking berries. These easy cheesecake parfaits are made with strawberry pie filling and are so simple to put together. Everything gets layered together in little jars for an incredible presentation.

INGREDIENTS

1 (8-ounce) package cream cheese, at room temperature

¼ cup powdered sugar

1 (21-ounce) can strawberry pie filling (page 26)

1 (8-ounce) container Cool Whip, thawed

2½ cups angel food cake cubes

6 fresh strawberry slices

INSTRUCTIONS

1. Beat the cream cheese until creamy. Add the powdered sugar and beat until smooth.

2. Spoon the pie filling into a large bowl. Use a knife and fork to cut the berries up into smaller chunks, if needed.

3. Add ½ cup of the pie filling to the cream cheese mixture and beat again.

4. Use a rubber spatula to fold 1½ cups of the Cool Whip gently into the cream cheese mixture.

5. Layer the cake cubes, strawberry cheesecake mixture, and the remainder of the pie filling, twice, into six 8-ounce canning jars.

6. Use a piping bag and icing tip 27 to swirl the remaining Cool Whip on top of the jars. Top each parfait with a fresh strawberry slice immediately before serving.

Note. Change out the strawberry pie filling for your favorite flavor.

No-Bake Raspberry Lemon Cream Cheesecake Parfaits

PREP TIME: 25 MINUTES | **SERVINGS:** MAKES SIX 8-OUNCE PARFAITS

The lemon mousse in these easy parfaits is good enough to eat alone. I kept digging my spoon into the bowl for another "taste test" before I layered everything into the jars. It's a wonder I had any cheesecake left to actually make parfaits with. The soft angel food cake, fresh juicy berries, and creamy lemon cheesecake mousse layered together made the dreamiest dessert. I couldn't wait to share these with my family after dinner.

INGREDIENTS

1 (8-ounce) package cream cheese, at room temperature

¼ cup powdered sugar

1 batch Lemon Curd (page 27)

3 cups cubed angel food cake

2 cups fresh raspberries

1 cup Cool Whip, thawed

6 lemon peel curls, for garnish

INSTRUCTIONS

1. Beat the cream cheese until creamy. Add the powdered sugar and beat until smooth.

2. Spoon in the lemon curd, a little at a time, and beat on low until very creamy.

3. Divide the cake cubes among six 8-ounce jars. Press the cake down to fill in all the open spaces in the bottoms of the jars.

4. Set aside 6 raspberries for garnish. Divide the remaining raspberries among the jars over the cake cubes.

5. Spoon the lemon cheesecake cream evenly over the berries. Tap the jars gently on the counter to settle all the layers.

6. Swirl the Cool Whip on top of the parfaits using a piping bag and icing tip 27. Top each swirl with a fresh raspberry and a lemon peel curl.

Note

» Layer graham cracker crumbs in the bottom of twelve small 4-ounce jelly jars, then top it with the lemon cream for a mini dessert.

» Layer everything into one large trifle bowl instead of assembling individual desserts.

No-Bake Mudslide Icebox Cake

PREP TIME: 20 MINUTES | SERVING: 9 SLICES

I am a huge fan of frozen ice cream drinks in the summer. I had my first mudslide drink one year when we were vacationing on a cruise. I cannot believe it took me that long to enjoy one. It's now one of my favorite drinks any time we go on vacation. That restaurant-style drink with coffee and chocolate was easy to transform into a no-bake cheesecake dessert. The chocolate graham crackers soften as the cheesecake mixture sets up, making the dessert taste just like a spiked ice cream sandwich. Yum!

INGREDIENTS

1 (8-ounce) package cream cheese, at room temperature

¼ cup sugar

3 ounces Kahlúa liqueur

3 ounces Baileys Irish Cream

1 (12-ounce) container Cool Whip, thawed

2 sleeves chocolate graham crackers

¼ cup hot fudge topping

INSTRUCTIONS

1. Beat the cream cheese and sugar until creamy. Add the Kahlúa and Baileys and beat until smooth. Gently fold in 3 cups of the Cool Whip using a rubber spatula.

2. Spread a thin layer of Cool Whip into the bottom of an 8-inch square baking dish with an offset spatula. Place a layer of chocolate graham crackers over the bottom of the pan.

3. Spread half the cheesecake batter evenly over the graham crackers. Place another layer of graham crackers over the cheesecake layer.

4. Spread the remaining cheesecake batter evenly over the crackers. Place one more layer of graham crackers on top of the cheesecake layer.

5. Spread the remaining Cool Whip on top of the graham crackers with an offset spatula. Refrigerate for at least 6 hours or overnight.

6. Place the hot fudge in a microwave-safe bowl and microwave for 15 to 20 seconds. Drizzle the hot fudge over the top of the cheesecake just before serving.

No-Bake Peanut Butter–Fluffernutter Cheesecake Pie

PREP TIME: 25 MINUTES | **SERVING:** 9 SLICES

One of my favorite things for lunches when I was growing up was a fluffernutter sandwich. For those of you who have never heard of a fluffernutter sandwich, I am so sorry. You have seriously missed out. This sandwich is made with white bread and smothered in peanut butter and marshmallow crème, and I would eat them over and over again each day. I introduced this fun sandwich to our kids when they were younger, and both our boys fell in love with the combo. They started taking them to school in their lunches, where they got a few of their friends hooked on the combo, too. This easy pie has a layer of peanut butter cheesecake and a layer of marshmallow cheesecake, just like my favorite sandwich. And of course, no peanut butter pie is complete until it is topped with lots of chopped up peanut butter cups! This pie didn't stand a chance in our fluffernutter-loving house.

INGREDIENTS

For the Crust

20 Oreo cookies

4 tablespoons (½ stick) unsalted butter, melted

For the Peanut Butter Cheesecake

1 (8-ounce) package cream cheese, at room temperature

½ cup powdered sugar

½ cup creamy peanut butter

1 cup Cool Whip, thawed

INSTRUCTIONS

1. **For the Crust:** Place the cookies, cream filling included, in a food processor. Pulse until the cookies become crumbs.

2. Mix together the cookie crumbs and melted butter. Press the mixture evenly into the bottom and sides of a 9-inch pie plate. Place the pie plate in the freezer while you make the fillings.

3. **For the Peanut Butter Cheesecake:** Beat the cream cheese until creamy. Add the powdered sugar and beat until smooth.

4. Add the peanut butter and beat until creamy.

5. Gently fold in the Cool Whip using a rubber spatula. Spread the filling evenly over the prepared crust.

For the Marshmallow Cheesecake

½ (4-ounce) package cream cheese, at room temperature

¾ cup marshmallow crème

1 cup Cool Whip, thawed

For the Topping

1 cup Cool Whip, thawed

2 cups chopped peanut butter cups

6. **For the Marshmallow Cheesecake:** Beat the cream cheese until creamy. Add the marshmallow crème and beat until smooth.

7. Gently fold in the Cool Whip with a clean rubber spatula. Spread the marshmallow cheesecake filling evenly over the peanut butter cheesecake layer in the pan.

8. **For the Topping:** Swirl the Cool Whip around the edges of the pie using a piping bag and icing tip 27. Sprinkle the peanut butter cups over the top of the cheesecake. Refrigerate until ready to serve.

No-Bake Banana–Chocolate Chip Cookie Icebox Cake

PREP TIME: 20 MINUTES | **SERVING:** MAKES ONE 8-INCH CHEESECAKE (10 SLICES)

Icebox cakes are another favorite dessert of mine to make. They are so easy to prepare and put together. The soft, creamy cheesecake layer comes together in minutes using just a few ingredients. Layer the creamy cheesecake filling with store-bought chocolate chip cookies in a pan, and then refrigerate it until it softens. A hot fudge drizzle, more cookie crumbles, and fresh banana slices are all you need to give it a fun decoration. I suggest doubling the ingredients and layering it in a 9 x 13-inch dish if you are serving a crowd. Just don't expect any leftovers to come home with you.

INGREDIENTS

1 (8-ounce) package cream cheese, at room temperature

¼ cup powdered sugar

1 teaspoon vanilla extract

1 cup mashed ripe banana

1 (16-ounce) container Cool Whip, thawed

1 (18-ounce) package crispy chocolate chip cookies (48)

¼ cup hot fudge topping

Fresh banana slices

INSTRUCTIONS

1. Beat the cream cheese until creamy. Add the powdered sugar and beat until smooth.

2. Add the vanilla and mashed banana and beat until creamy.

3. Gently fold in 4 cups of the Cool Whip with a rubber spatula.

4. Spread 2 tablespoons Cool Whip into the bottom of an 8-inch springform pan.

5. Place 12 cookies into the bottom of the pan. You may need to break and crumble a few to fit and fill in the bottom. Spread one-third of the cheesecake filling over the cookies.

6. Repeat the layers two more times. Place the remaining cookies on top of the cheesecake. Spread 1 cup Cool Whip over the cookies.

7. Cover and refrigerate the cheesecake for 4 to 6 hours or overnight.

8. Use a warm knife to run around the edge of the pan to loosen the cheesecake. Detach the springform pan and remove the cheesecake.

9. Pipe the remaining Cool Whip around the edge of the cheesecake using a piping bag and 1M icing tip.

10. Warm the hot fudge in the microwave until it is pourable. Drizzle the hot fudge over the top of the cake.

11. Right before serving, top the Cool Whip swirls with fresh banana slices.

No-Bake Chocolate Strawberry Cheesecake Trifle

PREP TIME: 40 MINUTES | SERVING: MAKES ONE LARGE TRIFLE (15 SERVINGS)

If you enjoy desserts with different textures and flavors, a dessert trifle is just what you need in your life. This trifle has layers of crunchy cookies, creamy cheesecake, and fresh berries. It is a flavor explosion in your mouth with every bite. You could also get creative and use vanilla cookies for a Neapolitan trifle. Or use banana slices instead of strawberries for a whole new flavor combo. So grab a spoon and get ready to dig in.

INGREDIENTS

For the Cheesecake

2 (8-ounce) packages cream cheese, at room temperature

¼ cup sugar

1 (7-ounce) jar marshmallow crème

½ cup milk

8 ounces semisweet baking chocolate, melted

1 (8-ounce) container Cool Whip, thawed

For the Layers

45 Oreo cookies, chopped into large chunks

5 cups sliced strawberries

8 whole strawberries

8 mini Oreo cookies

INSTRUCTIONS

1. **For the Cheesecake:** Beat the cream cheese until creamy. Add the sugar and beat until smooth.

2. Add the marshmallow crème and beat until creamy. Slowly beat in the milk until the mixture is smooth again.

3. Spoon in the melted chocolate and beat until completely incorporated.

4. Gently fold in 2 cups of the Cool Whip with a rubber spatula.

5. **For the Layers:** Place half the cookie chunks in the bottom of a large trifle bowl. Spoon half the cheesecake filling over the cookies. Use the back of a spoon to smooth the cheesecake out and make it flat in the bowl.

6. Place a few sliced strawberries standing up around the edge of the bowl. Place half the sliced strawberries lying flat over the cheesecake layer.

7. Repeat the layers, ending with the strawberries on top.

8. Place the whole strawberries around the top and pipe the remaining Cool Whip in between the berries using a piping bag and icing tip 27. Top each Cool Whip swirl with a mini Oreo cookie.

Note. This trifle is best served the day it is made.

No-Bake Hot Fudge Cheesecake Parfaits

PREP TIME: 20 MINUTES | **SERVING:** MAKES 4 LARGE PARFAITS

What could be better than getting your own jar of cheesecake? I love making individual desserts because everyone enjoys getting their own personal treat after dinner. These little parfaits are just three layers of goodness, plus a creamy topping. Chocolate cookie crumbs add a little crust to the bottom of the jar, and then you add layers of hot fudge and vanilla cheesecakes into the jars. An easy, peasy dessert in just minutes.

INGREDIENTS

For the Crust
10 Oreo cookies

For the Hot Fudge Cheesecake
1 (8-ounce) package cream cheese, at room temperature

¾ cup hot fudge topping

½ teaspoon vanilla extract

2 tablespoons milk

1 cup Cool Whip, thawed

For the White Chocolate Cheesecake
1 (8-ounce) package cream cheese, at room temperature

3 ounces white baking chocolate, melted

½ teaspoon vanilla extract

2 tablespoons milk

1 cup Cool Whip, thawed

For the Topping
1 cup Cool Whip, thawed

4 maraschino cherries with stems, patted dry

INSTRUCTIONS

1. **For the Crust:** Place the cookies, cream filling included, in a food processor. Pulse the cookies until they become crumbs.

2. Reserve 1 tablespoon cookie crumbs for later. Divide the remaining cookie crumbs evenly among four large parfait glasses. Set the glasses aside.

3. **For the Hot Fudge Cheesecake:** Beat the cream cheese until creamy. Add the hot fudge and beat until smooth.

4. Add the milk and vanilla and beat until creamy. Gently fold in the Cool Whip with a rubber spatula.

5. Spoon the mixture evenly over the cookie crumbs in the glasses. Use the back of the spoon to smooth it out and make it level.

6. **For the White Chocolate Cheesecake:** Beat the cream cheese until creamy. Add the melted white chocolate and beat until smooth.

7. Add the milk and vanilla and beat until creamy. Gently fold in the Cool Whip with a rubber spatula.

8. Spoon the mixture into the parfait glasses and use the back of the spoon to smooth it out.

9. <u>For the Topping:</u> Top each glass with a Cool Whip swirl using a piping bag and 1M icing tip. Sprinkle the reserved cookie crumbs on top, then place a cherry on top of each.

Note. These cheesecake layers could be divided into eight small 4-ounce jelly jars, if you wanted to make even smaller desserts.

5

Cheesecake Brownies

×

OH YEAH!

I don't know about you, but I crave multiple desserts all
the time. So what's a girl to do? Eat them all!
By combining brownies and cheesecake, I can enjoy two
desserts at once, without feeling guilty for grabbing
another dessert. It's the ultimate win-win when you can
have a slice of Cherry Chocolate Cheesecake
Brownies (page 152) or any of these other amazing
combinations after dinner.

Coconut Cream Cheesecake Brownies

PREP TIME: 30 MINUTES | **BAKE TIME:** 48 TO 50 MINUTES | **SERVING:** MAKES 24 BARS

The only thing better than a dark chocolate fudgy brownie is that same brownie topped with a coconut cheesecake layer and chocolate. This is one brownie that I have to share with someone else right away because chocolate and coconut is something I could eat all day long. One little sliver every hour seems to be how I like to enjoy my cheesecake brownies. My jeans, on the other hand, do not agree with this eating habit. Thank goodness for CrossFit!

INGREDIENTS

1 Double Batch Brownie batter (page 21)

For the Cheesecake

1 (8-ounce) package cream cheese, at room temperature

2 tablespoons unsalted butter, at room temperature

1 tablespoon cornstarch

1 (14-ounce) can sweetened condensed milk

½ teaspoon coconut extract

½ teaspoon rum extract

1 large egg

2 cups sweetened shredded coconut

For the Topping

¼ cup heavy cream

2 tablespoons unsalted butter

¾ cup dark chocolate chips

INSTRUCTIONS

1. Preheat the oven to 350°F. Line a 9 x 13-inch baking pan with aluminum foil and spray it with nonstick baking spray. Spread the brownie batter in the prepared pan. Set aside.

2. For the Cheesecake: Beat the cream cheese until creamy. Add the butter and cornstarch and beat again.

3. Add the condensed milk and extracts. Beat until smooth and creamy. Use a wire whisk attachment, if needed.

4. Add the egg and beat until incorporated. Do not overbeat the batter. Stir the shredded coconut into the cheesecake.

5. Gently spoon the cheesecake batter over the brownie batter in the pan.

6. Bake the cheesecake brownies for 48 to 50 minutes.

7. Remove the pan from the oven and place it on a wire rack. Let the cheesecake cool for 1 hour, then refrigerate it for 3 to 4 hours, or until completely chilled.

8. For the Topping: Place the cream, butter, and chocolate chips in a microwave-safe bowl. Microwave for 20–30 seconds. Stir the chocolate until melted and creamy. Spread the chocolate on top of the chilled cheesecake with an offset spatula.

Coffee Cookies-and-Cream Cheesecake Brownie Cake

PREP TIME: 45 MINUTES | **BAKE TIME:** 27 TO 28 MINUTES | **SERVING:** MAKES ONE 9-INCH CHEESECAKE (12 SLICES)

Years ago, my husband and I found a pack of Oreo cookies filled with a coffee cream center. I can't tell you how many packages of those cookies we went through in just one month. Seriously, they were amazing. One sad day, we couldn't find them. It turns out they were just a specialty flavor available for a very short time. Every time I make a dessert that includes coffee and Oreo cookies, my husband and I look at each other and say, "Do you remember those cookies?" If you never had those coffee cookies, this brownie cake will give you a taste of what I'm talking about. The creamy coffee cheesecake is loaded with chocolate cookie chunks, and then it is spread on top of a chewy brownie crust. It's a dessert dream!

INGREDIENTS

1 Single-Batch Brownie batter (page 20)

For the Cheesecake

1 (8-ounce) package cream cheese, at room temperature

¼ cup sugar

2 teaspoons instant coffee granules

2 tablespoons hot water

1 (16-ounce) container Cool Whip, thawed

21 Oreo cookies, chopped into chunks

INSTRUCTIONS

1. Preheat the oven to 350°F. Line a 9-inch springform pan with parchment paper.

2. Spread the brownie batter into the bottom of the pan. Bake the brownie for 27 to 28 minutes.

3. Remove the pan from the oven and let the brownie cool completely. Run a sharp knife around the edge of the brownie to loosen it from the pan.

4. Detach the springform pan ring to loosen it. Place another sheet of parchment paper and a plate on top of the brownie. Flip it over and peel the parchment paper off the bottom of the brownie. Place the bottom of the springform pan over the brownie and flip it right-side up again. Place the springform pan ring back on the pan with the brownie inside.

5. **For the Cheesecake:** Beat the cream cheese until creamy. Add the sugar and beat until smooth.

(continued)

6. Dissolve the coffee granules in the hot water. Add the coffee to the cream cheese and beat until creamy.

7. Gently fold in 3 cups of the Cool Whip with a rubber spatula. Set the bowl aside.

8. Gently stir 2 cups of the cookie chunks into the cheesecake mixture.

9. Spread the cheesecake mixture evenly over the cooled brownie in the pan. Refrigerate for 2 to 3 hours, or until set.

10. Spread the remaining 3 cups of Cool Whip evenly over the top of the cheesecake. Run a sharp knife under hot water and dry it off. Run the knife around the edge of the cheesecake to loosen it from the pan before removing the springform pan ring again. Place the brownie cheesecake on a plate.

11. Sprinkle the remaining cookie chunks over the top of the cheesecake before serving.

Coconut Cheesecake Brownie Trifle

PREP TIME: 45 MINUTES | **BAKE TIME:** 30 MINUTES | **SERVING:** MAKES ONE LARGE TRIFLE (15 SERVINGS)

Trifles are a fun dessert to make when you need to take something with you to a party. They look impressive and fancy, but trifles are really quite easy to put together. If you love chocolate and coconut, you are going to love the layers in this cheesecake trifle. Homemade brownie chunks, creamy chocolate cheesecake, fluffy coconut cheesecake, and lots of toasted coconut will satisfy your sweet tooth with every bite. Putting this creation into a clear glass trifle bowl will make you pause before scooping into it because of how pretty it is. But only a short pause, because it is well worth digging into.

INGREDIENTS

1 Double-Batch Brownies, baked and cooled (page 21)

For the Coconut Cheesecake

1 (8-ounce) package cream cheese, at room temperature

½ cup cream of coconut

½ cup marshmallow crème

½ teaspoon rum extract

2 cups Cool Whip, thawed

1 cup sweetened shredded coconut

For the Chocolate Cheesecake

2 (8-ounce) packages cream cheese, at room temperature

1 cup hot fudge topping

2 cups Cool Whip, thawed

For the Topping

¼ cup Toasted Coconut (page 30)

1½ cups Cool Whip, thawed

Chocolate-covered coffee beans

INSTRUCTIONS

1. Cut the brownie into 1-inch squares. Set the brownie cubes aside.

2. **For the Coconut Cheesecake:** Beat the cream cheese until creamy. Add the cream of coconut and beat until smooth.

3. Add the marshmallow crème and rum extract and beat until creamy. Fold in the Cool Whip with a rubber spatula, and then gently stir in the shredded coconut. Set aside.

4. **For the Chocolate Cheesecake:** Beat the cream cheese until creamy. Add the hot fudge and beat until smooth.

5. Gently fold in the Cool Whip with a rubber spatula.

6. **Assembly:** Place half the brownie cubes in the bottom of a large trifle bowl.

7. Spoon half the hot fudge cheesecake batter on top of the brownies. Use the back of the spoon to spread it out evenly.

(continued)

8. Place all the coconut cheesecake batter in the bowl over the hot fudge cheesecake. Spread it out evenly with a spatula.

9. Add the remaining brownie cubes on top of the coconut layer.

10. Spread the remaining hot fudge cheesecake filling over the brownies. Use the back of the spoon to spread it out evenly.

11. <u>For the Topping:</u> Sprinkle the top of the cheesecake with the toasted coconut.

12. Swirl the Cool Whip around the edges of the trifle using a piping bag and 1M icing tip. Top the swirls with the coffee beans.

White Chocolate Raspberry Cheesecake Brownies

PREP TIME: 30 MINUTES	BAKE TIME: 50 TO 55 MINUTES	SERVING: MAKES 24 BARS

Fresh raspberries do not stand a chance in our house. Every time I bring them home from the store, my family pounces on them. When I have a recipe idea that calls for raspberries, I buy extra berries for my family to nibble on while I bake with the rest. These cheesecake brownies were one that I had to make sure the berries lasted long enough for. The layers of white chocolate cheesecake with the pops of red berries throughout are so pretty on top of these dark chocolate brownies. Not only do they look incredible, but the flavor combination is out of this world!

INGREDIENTS

1 Double Batch Brownie batter (page 21)

For the Cheesecake
2 (8-ounce) packages cream cheese, at room temperature

¼ cup sugar

¼ cup sour cream

1 teaspoon vanilla extract

8 ounces white baking chocolate, melted

2 large eggs

1½ cups fresh raspberries

INSTRUCTIONS

1. Preheat the oven to 350°F. Line a 9 x 13-inch baking pan with aluminum foil and spray it with nonstick baking spray.

2. Spread the brownie batter into the bottom of the prepared pan. Set aside.

3. **For the Cheesecake:** Beat the cream cheese until creamy. Add the sugar, sour cream, and vanilla and beat until smooth.

4. Add the melted white chocolate and beat until creamy.

5. Add the eggs one at a time, beating well after each addition. Make sure the eggs are fully incorporated, but do not overbeat the batter.

6. Stir the raspberries very carefully into the cheesecake batter. Spoon the cheesecake batter gently over the brownie batter. Spread the batter out to the edges of the pan so that no brownie batter is showing.

7. Bake the cheesecake for 50 to 55 minutes.

8. Remove the pan from the oven and place it on a wire rack. Let the cheesecake cool for 1 hour, and refrigerate it for 4 hours, or until completely chilled.

Cherry Chocolate Cheesecake Brownies

PREP TIME: 3 HOURS 45 MINUTES | **BAKE TIME:** 45 TO 48 MINUTES | **SERVING:** MAKES 24 BARS

A few years ago, I made these brownies and shared them with a group of friends at a dinner party. One of the younger boys asked what the dessert was called. When he heard they were just cheesecake brownies, he shook his head and said that they should be called a slice of heaven because they tasted so good. I have to admit that after one bite of the chocolate cherry cheesecake goodness, I agreed wholeheartedly with him. The creamy layers taste absolutely heavenly together!

INGREDIENTS

1 Double-Batch Homemade Brownie batter (page 21)

For the Cheesecake:

2 (8-ounce) packages cream cheese, at room temperature

½ cup sugar

1 teaspoon vanilla extract

¼ cup sour cream

4 ounces semisweet baking chocolate, melted

2 large eggs

For the Topping

1 (8-ounce) container Cool Whip, thawed

1 (21-ounce) can cherry pie filling (page 26)

INSTRUCTIONS

1. Preheat the oven to 350°F. Line a 9 x 13-inch baking pan with aluminum foil and spray it with nonstick baking spray.

2. Spread the brownie batter into the bottom of the prepared pan. Set aside.

3. **For the Cheesecake:** Beat the cream cheese until creamy. Add the sugar, vanilla, and sour cream and beat until smooth.

4. Add the melted chocolate and beat until completely incorporated.

5. Add the eggs one a time, beating well after each addition. Make sure the eggs are fully incorporated, but do not overbeat the batter.

6. Spoon the cheesecake batter gently on top of the brownie batter. Spread it out evenly to the edges of the pan, making sure all the brownie batter is covered.

7. Bake the cheesecake for 45 to 48 minutes.

8. Remove the pan from the oven and place it on a wire rack. Let the cheesecake cool for 1 hour, then refrigerate it for 3 to 4 hours, or until completely chilled.

9. <u>**For the Topping:**</u> Spread the Cool Whip on top of the chilled cheesecake using an offset spatula. Gently spoon the pie filling on top of the Cool Whip.

Note. Use strawberry pie filling if you prefer that instead.

Peppermint Swirl Cheesecake Brownies

PREP TIME: 40 MINUTES | **BAKE TIME:** 45 TO 48 MINUTES | **SERVING:** MAKES 24 BARS

When the Christmas holiday starts getting closer, I get excited to bake all the things with peppermint added to them. Cookies, cakes, brownies, and fudge have all been given the peppermint treatment over the years. The peppermint cheesecake on top of these home-made brownies has a fun red-and-white swirl. I like to serve these cheesecake squares with a big swirl of Cool Whip and more peppermint candy bits! Sing with me, "It's beginning to look a lot like Christmas, with every bite you take."

INGREDIENTS

1 Double-Batch Homemade Brownie batter (page 21)

For the Cheesecake

2 (8-ounce) packages cream cheese, at room temperature

½ cup granulated sugar

¼ cup heavy cream

2 teaspoons peppermint extract

2 tablespoons all-purpose flour

2 large eggs

Red or pink gel food coloring

2 tablespoons peppermint candy bits

For Serving

1½ cups Cool Whip, thawed

¼ cup peppermint candy bits (optional)

INSTRUCTIONS

1. Preheat the oven to 350°F. Line a 9 x 13-inch baking pan with aluminum foil and spray it with nonstick baking spray.

2. Spread the brownie batter into the bottom of the pre-pared pan. Set aside.

3. **For the Cheesecake:** Beat the cream cheese until creamy. Add the sugar, cream, peppermint extract, and flour and beat until smooth.

4. Add the eggs one at a time, beating well after each addition. Make sure the eggs are fully incorporated, but do not overbeat the batter.

5. Spoon 1 cup of the cheesecake batter into a separate bowl. Use the gel food coloring to tint the batter to your desired red or pink color. Stir in the peppermint candy bits.

6. Spread the white cheesecake batter evenly over the brownie batter. Drop the red or pink cheesecake batter randomly over the top. Use a butter knife to gently swirl the mixture. Do not let the knife go through to the brownie layer.

7. Bake the cheesecake for 45 to 48 minutes.

8. Remove the pan from the oven and place it on a wire rack. Let the cheesecake cool for 1 hour, then refrigerate it for 3 to 4 hours, or until completely chilled.

9. Serve the cheesecake brownies with the Cool Whip and additional peppermint bits on top, if desired.

Cookie Dough Cheesecake Brownie Cake

PREP TIME: 40 MINUTES | **BAKE TIME:** 27 MINUTES | **SERVING:** MAKES ONE 9-INCH CHEESECAKE (12 SLICES)

This fun cheesecake is one of my favorite recipes that I have ever shared on the blog. I just love finding ways to combine three desserts into one fun and amazing treat! The creamy, no-bake cheesecake is loaded with little cookie dough bites and is placed on a chewy brownie crust. The combination of all three will have you licking your lips!

INGREDIENTS

1 Single-Batch Homemade Brownie batter (page 20)

For the Cheesecake

1 (8-ounce) package cream cheese, at room temperature

¼ cup packed brown sugar

1 teaspoon vanilla extract

1 (12-ounce) container Cool Whip, thawed

1 batch Cookie Dough Bites (page 23), frozen

For the Topping

¼ cup mini chocolate chips

INSTRUCTIONS

1. Preheat the oven to 350°F. Line a 9-inch springform pan with parchment paper.

2. Spread the brownie batter into the prepared pan. Bake the brownie for 27 minutes. Remove the pan from the oven and let the brownie cool completely.

3. Run a sharp knife around the edge of the brownie to loosen it from the pan. Open the springform pan ring. Place a clean sheet of parchment and a plate on the brownie and flip it over. Peel off the baked-on parchment. Flip the brownie back over onto the springform pan bottom and put the ring back on with the brownie inside. Set aside.

4. **For the Cheesecake:** Beat the cream cheese until creamy. Add the brown sugar and vanilla and beat until smooth.

5. Gently fold in 3 cups of the Cool Whip using a rubber spatula.

6. Cut the frozen cookie dough bites in half. Place 20 cookie dough halves on a plate and put the plate back in the freezer. Gently stir the rest of the cookie dough bites into the cheesecake mixture.

7. Spoon the cheesecake filing over the brownie crust and spread it out evenly with a spatula. Refrigerate the cheesecake for at least 1 hour.

8. Run a knife around the edge of the pan to loosen the cheesecake from the pan. Detach the springform pan ring and remove the cheesecake from the pan. Place the brownie cheesecake on a serving plate.

9. Swirl the remaining Cool Whip around the edges with a piping bag and 1M icing tip.

10. Place the reserved frozen cookie dough halves on top of the swirls. Sprinkle the mini chocolate chips in the center of the cheesecake.

Peanut Butter Cup Cheesecake Brownies

PREP TIME: 40 MINUTES | **BAKE TIME:** 45 MINUTES | **SERVING:** MAKES 24 BARS

I could eat chocolate and peanut butter every day of my life. One bite of this combo, and I am a goner. This rich and decadent brownie dessert got rave reviews from our oldest son after he tried them. Homemade chocolate brownies swirled with peanut butter cheesecake and then topped with melted chocolate and peanut butter cups will satisfy that peanut butter and chocolate sweet tooth in no time at all. Just make sure you have a big glass of milk ready!

INGREDIENTS

1 Double-Batch Brownie batter (page 21; use regular cocoa powder)

For the Cheesecake

1 (8-ounce) package cream cheese, at room temperature

½ cup sugar

2 tablespoons sour cream

½ teaspoon vanilla extract

¼ cup creamy peanut butter

1 large egg

For the Topping

¼ cup heavy cream

2 tablespoons unsalted butter

¾ cup milk chocolate chips

1½ cups chopped peanut butter cups

INSTRUCTIONS

1. Preheat the oven to 350°F. Line a 9 x 13-inch baking pan with aluminum foil and spray it with nonstick baking spray.

2. Reserve ½ cup of the brownie batter. Spread the rest of the brownie batter into the bottom of the prepared pan. Set aside.

3. For the Cheesecake: Beat the cream cheese until creamy. Add the sugar and beat until smooth.

4. Add the sour cream, vanilla, and peanut butter and beat until creamy.

5. Add the egg and beat until fully incorporated. Do not overbeat the batter.

6. Spread the cheesecake batter over the top of the brownie batter, making sure to cover all of the brownie batter.

7. Drop the reserved brownie batter over the top of the cheesecake. Use a butter knife to gently swirl them together.

8. Bake the cheesecake for 45 minutes.

9. Remove the pan from the oven and place it on a wire rack. Let the cheesecake cool for 1 hour, then refrigerate it for 4 hours, or until completely chilled.

10. For the Topping: Place the cream, butter, and chocolate chips in a microwave-safe bowl. Microwave for 20 to 30 seconds. Stir the chocolate until melted and creamy. Heat for an additional 15 seconds, if needed.

11. Spread the melted chocolate over the chilled cheesecake with an offset spatula. Sprinkle the peanut butter cups on top of the chocolate while it is still wet. Refrigerate the cheesecake until the chocolate is set.

6

Cheesecake Pies

×

SHEER AWESOMENESS!!!

Cheesecake and pie were meant to be together. This is just a fact of life. A big slice of Apple Crumb Cheesecake Pie (page 168) with a hot cup of coffee just screams comfort food to me. And I especially love how easy it is to combine two of your favorite desserts into one amazing dessert and how much fun you can have pairing flavors together! They are also perfect for parties—just be ready for the *oohs* and *aahs* when people realize you've combined their two favorite desserts!

Snickers Cheesecake Pie

PREP TIME: 30 MINUTES | **BAKE TIME:** 40 MINUTES | **SERVING:** MAKES ONE 10-INCH PIE (12 SLICES)

What do you get when you combine caramel cheesecake with candy bars, chocolate, and caramel drizzles? You get an amazing dessert that everyone will be drooling over. The layer of creamy cheesecake contrasts with the crunchy peanuts in the candy bars. This is a very rich dessert, but totally worth every single bite! Don't be afraid to experiment a little with this one. Feel free to swap out the Snickers for another candy bar that you enjoy. There are so many amazing candy bars that can turn this one recipe into an infinite number of candy creations!

INGREDIENTS

For the Crust

20 Oreo cookies

4 tablespoons (½ stick) unsalted butter, melted

For the Cheesecake

2 (8-ounce) packages cream cheese, at room temperature

⅔ cup packed brown sugar

¼ cup sour cream

¼ cup Caramel Topping (page 25)

2 tablespoons all-purpose flour

2 large eggs

1 cup chopped Snickers candy bars

For the Topping

¼ cup heavy cream

1 cup milk chocolate chips

1 (8-ounce) container Cool Whip, thawed

¼ cup Caramel Topping (page 25)

1 cup chopped Snickers candy bars

INSTRUCTIONS

1. Place a baking sheet on the very bottom rack of the oven and fill it halfway with water. Preheat the oven to 350°F.

2. **For the Crust:** Place the cookies, cream filling included, in a food processor. Pulse the cookies until they become crumbs.

3. Mix together the cookie crumbs and melted butter. Press the crumbs firmly into the bottom and sides of a 10-inch deep-dish pie plate. Refrigerate until ready to use.

4. **For the Cheesecake:** Beat the cream cheese until creamy. Add the brown sugar and beat the mixture until smooth.

5. Add the sour cream, caramel topping, and flour and beat until creamy.

6. Add the eggs one a time, beating well after addition. Make sure the eggs are fully incorporated, but do not overbeat the batter.

(continued)

7. Gently stir in the candy bar chunks by hand. Spoon the cheesecake batter into the prepared crust.

8. Place the pie plate on the oven rack right above the tray of water. Bake the cheesecake for 40 to 45 minutes.

9. Remove the pie plate from the oven and place it on a wire rack. Let the cheesecake cool for 1 hour, then refrigerate it for 2 to 3 hours, or until completely chilled.

10. <u>**For the Topping:**</u> Place the cream and chocolate chips in a microwave safe bowl. Microwave for 20 to 30 seconds. Stir the chocolate until melted and creamy. Heat for an additional 15 seconds, if needed.

11. Spread the melted chocolate over the chilled cheesecake with an offset spatula. Refrigerate the cheesecake until the chocolate is set.

12. Spread the Cool Whip over the chocolate with the offset spatula. Drizzle the caramel over the Cool Whip and sprinkle the chopped candy bars on top.

Funfetti Cheesecake Pie

PREP TIME: 30 MINUTES   BAKE TIME: 30 MINUTES   SERVING: MAKES ONE 9-INCH PIE (10 SLICES)

Everyone loves sprinkles. Well, unless you are my husband and sons. They will always brush the sprinkles off the tops of cookies or cake instead of eating the colored bits. I think they might be aliens, because who doesn't like a generous helping of happiness? This creamy cheesecake pie is loaded with sprinkles in every single layer, and then another layer of sprinkles goes on the very top. This pie would be a great dessert option for parties or birthdays. You could customize the colors of the sprinkles to match your party décor. How fun would that be?

INGREDIENTS

Dough for 1 Piecrust (page 22)

For the Cheesecake

1 (8-ounce) package cream cheese, at room temperature

¼ cup sugar

½ teaspoon vanilla extract

1 large egg

2 tablespoons rainbow jimmies

For the Mousse

1 (8-ounce) cream cheese, at room temperature

¼ cup sugar

½ teaspoon vanilla extract

1 batch Whipped Cream (page 29)

4 tablespoons rainbow jimmies

INSTRUCTIONS

1. Place a large rimmed baking sheet on the very bottom rack of the oven and fill it halfway with water. Heat the oven to 350°F. Spray a 9-inch pie plate with nonstick baking spray.

2. Roll out the pie dough on a floured surface and place it in the prepared pie plate. Fold the edges under and crimp the dough. Refrigerate until ready to use.

3. **For the Cheesecake:** Beat the cream cheese until creamy. Add the sugar and vanilla and beat until smooth.

4. Add the egg and beat until fully incorporated. Do not overbeat the batter. Gently stir in the sprinkles by hand.

5. Pour the cheesecake batter into the prepared pie crust.

6. Place the pie plate on the oven rack right above the tray of water. Bake the cheesecake pie for 30 minutes. The cheesecake may be slightly puffed up, but it will flatten out as it cools.

7. Remove the pie plate from the oven and place it on a wire rack. Let the cheesecake pie cool for 1 hour, then refrigerate it for 2 to 3 hours, or until completely chilled.

(continued)

8. <u>**For the Mousse:**</u> Beat the cream cheese until creamy. Add the sugar and vanilla and beat until smooth.

9. Reserve ½ cup of the whipped cream. Gently fold the remaining whipped cream into the cheesecake filling using a rubber spatula. Stir 2 tablespoons of the sprinkles into the filling. Spread the mixture evenly on top of the chilled cheesecake with an offset spatula.

10. Sprinkle the remaining 2 tablespoons sprinkles over the cheesecake. Swirl the reserved whipped cream around the edge of the cheesecake using a piping bag and icing tip 27.

Apple Crumb Cheesecake Pie

PREP TIME: 35 MINUTES | BAKE TIME: 40 MINUTES | SERVING: MAKES ONE 9-INCH PIE (10 SLICES)

A few years ago I made and posted this apple cheesecake pie on the blog, and it was an instant favorite with our readers. After all, apple pie is the all-American dessert! Some people top apple pie with ice cream; I chose to combine it with a cheesecake. This time I gave this delicious pie a little bit of a twist by adding crumbs to the top of the apples before baking it. It was so good that I will be adding that buttery crumb topping every single time from now on. And, of course, drizzling homemade caramel topping on top is always a must! For a triple dose of amazingness, feel free to top it with some ice cream, too!

INGREDIENTS

Dough for 1 Piecrust (page 22)

For the Cheesecake

1 (8-ounce) package cream cheese, at room temperature

¼ cup granulated sugar

1 large egg

3 cups Apple Pie Filling (page 28)

For the Crumb Topping

¼ cup all-purpose flour

¼ cup quick-cooking oats

¼ cup packed brown sugar

½ teaspoon ground cinnamon

¼ teaspoon ground nutmeg

2 tablespoons unsalted butter, melted

Vanilla ice cream, for serving (optional)

¼ cup Caramel Topping (page 25), for serving (optional)

INSTRUCTIONS

1. Preheat the oven to 375°F. Spray a 9-inch pie plate with nonstick baking spray.

2. Place the dough in the pie plate. Fold the edges of the dough under and crimp them. Refrigerate until ready to use.

3. _For the Cheesecake:_ Beat the cream cheese until creamy. Add the granulated sugar and beat the mixture until smooth.

4. Add the egg and beat until fully incorporated. Do not overbeat the batter.

5. Spread the cheesecake batter in the prepared pie crust. Gently spoon the apple pie filling on top of the cheese-cake batter.

6. _For the Crumb Topping:_ Mix together the crumb topping ingredients. Sprinkle the mixture evenly over the apple pie filling.

7. Bake the cheesecake pie for 40 minutes. Remove the pie plate from the oven and place it on a wire rack. Let the cheesecake pie cool for 1 hour, then refrigerate it for 2 to 3 hours, or until completely chilled.

8. Serve the slices of cheesecake pie with vanilla ice cream and caramel topping, if desired.

Pecan Cheesecake Pie

PREP TIME: 25 MINUTES | BAKE TIME: 50 TO 55 MINUTES | SERVING: MAKES ONE 9-INCH PIE (10 SLICES)

Pecans and cheesecake were meant to be together. My husband came up with the idea to bake cheesecake and pecan pie together a few years ago when we wanted something different after our Thanksgiving dinner. This recipe was an instant favorite with readers when we shared it on the blog. Amazing and magical things happen in the oven while this pie bakes. The gooey caramel layer sinks to the bottom while leaving the pecans to bake on top of the cheesecake. Every single time we make this cheesecake pie, it disappears within minutes.

INGREDIENTS

Dough for 1 Piecrust (page 22)

For the Cheesecake

1 (8-ounce) package cream cheese, at room temperature

¼ cup sugar

1 large egg

For the Pecan Layer

⅔ cup dark corn syrup

2 large eggs

⅔ cup sugar

1 tablespoon unsalted butter, melted

½ teaspoon vanilla extract

1 cup pecan halves

INSTRUCTIONS

1. Preheat the oven to 350°F. Spray a 9-inch pie plate with nonstick baking spray.

2. Roll the dough out on a floured surface and place it in the pie plate. Fold the edges under and crimp the dough. Refrigerate until ready to use.

3. **For the Cheesecake:** Beat the cream cheese until creamy. Add the sugar and beat the mixture until smooth.

4. Add the egg and beat until fully incorporated. Do not overbeat the batter. Spread the cheesecake over the bottom of the prepared pie crust.

5. **For the Pecan Layer:** Whisk together the corn syrup, eggs, sugar, butter, and vanilla in a bowl. Stir in the pecans.

6. Spoon the pecan mixture over the cheesecake layer gently.

7. Cover the edges of the pie crust with aluminum foil. Bake the cheesecake pie for 50 to 55 minutes.

8. Remove the pie plate from the oven and place it on a wire rack. Let the pie cool for 1 hour, then refrigerate it for 2 to 3 hours, or until completely chilled.

Chocolate Coconut Cream Cheesecake Tart

PREP TIME: 40 MINUTES   **BAKE TIME:** 38 MINUTES   **SERVING:** MAKES ONE 9-INCH TART (10 SLICES)

They say you eat with your eyes first. Over the years, I have realized that I love to bake desserts that have layers in them. There is something so satisfying about cutting into a pie or cake and seeing the different colors and textures. This cheesecake tart is one of those desserts that I cut into and then stood back to admire. The dark cookie crust, chocolate cheesecake, and coconut no-bake cheesecake layers were so pretty that I almost didn't want to dig in. Yeah, right. You don't believe that for a minute, do you?

INGREDIENTS

For the Crust

20 Oreo cookies

4 tablespoons (½ stick) unsalted butter, melted

For the Chocolate Cheesecake

1 (8-ounce) package cream cheese, at room temperature

¼ cup sugar

⅓ cup sour cream

½ teaspoon vanilla extract

4 ounces semisweet baking chocolate, melted

1 large egg

INSTRUCTIONS

1. Preheat the oven to 350°F.

2. **For the Crust:** Place the cookies, cream filling included, in a food processor. Pulse the cookies until they become crumbs.

3. Stir together the cookie crumbs and melted butter. Press the mixture firmly into the bottom and sides of a 9-inch tart pan.

4. Bake the crust for 8 minutes. Remove the pan from the oven and let cool. Keep the oven on.

5. Place a large rimmed baking sheet on the very bottom rack of the oven and fill it halfway with water.

6. **For the Chocolate Cheesecake:** Beat the cream cheese until creamy. Add the sugar, sour cream, and vanilla and beat until smooth.

7. Add the melted chocolate and beat until completely incorporated.

For the Coconut Cheesecake

1 (8-ounce) package cream cheese, at room temperature

¼ cup sugar

½ teaspoon coconut extract

½ teaspoon rum extract

1 cup sweetened shredded coconut

1 (8-ounce) container Cool Whip, thawed

For the Topping

½ cup Toasted Coconut (page 30)

8. Add the egg and beat until fully incorporated. Do not overbeat the batter. Spread the cheesecake batter over the cooled crust.

9. Place the pie plate on the oven rack right above the tray of water. Bake the cheesecake pie for 30 minutes.

10. Remove the pie plate from the oven and place it on a wire rack. Let the pie cool for 1 hour, then refrigerate it for 2 to 3 hours, or until completely chilled.

11. For the Coconut Cheesecake: Beat the cream cheese until creamy. Add the sugar and extracts and beat until smooth.

12. Stir the shredded coconut into the cheesecake mixture by hand. Gently fold in 2 cups of the Cool Whip with a rubber spatula. Spread the coconut cheesecake filling on top of the chilled chocolate cheesecake layer.

13. For the Topping: Sprinkle the toasted coconut all over the top of the cheesecake. Swirl the remaining Cool Whip around the edge of the tart using a piping bag and icing tip 27.

Mini Orange Cream Cheesecake Pies

PREP TIME: 30 MINUTES | **BAKE TIME:** 15 MINUTES | **SERVING:** MAKES 12 MINI TARTS

One fun drink that my husband likes to enjoy during the summer is a scoop of vanilla ice cream blended with orange juice. Since I love combining two desserts into one sweet treat, I knew that I wanted to make a cheesecake pie that included the orange and vanilla flavor from this drink. The result was a cute little tart that my husband said were similar to those icy summer drinks.

INGREDIENTS

Dough for 1 Piecrust (page 22)

For the Cheesecake:

1 (8-ounce) package cream cheese, at room temperature

½ cup sugar

1 teaspoon orange extract

1 large egg

For the Topping

1 batch Whipped Cream (page 29)

1 small can mandarin oranges, drained and patted dry

INSTRUCTIONS

1. Preheat the oven to 375°F.

2. Roll out the pie dough on a floured surface. Cut out as many 3-inch circles as you can. Reroll the dough to cut more circles until you have 12 circles. Press one circle into each cavity of a 12-cavity mini-tart pan. Refrigerate until ready to use.

3. **For the Cheesecake:** Beat the cream cheese until creamy. Add the sugar and orange extract and beat until smooth.

4. Add the egg and beat until fully incorporated. Do not overbeat the batter. Spoon the cheesecake evenly into the prepared pie crusts.

5. Bake for 15 to 17 minutes.

6. Remove the pan from the oven and place it on a wire rack. Let the cheesecakes cool in the pan for 15 minutes, then gently remove them from the pan and place them on the wire rack.

7. Let the cheesecakes cool for 45 minutes, then refrigerate them for 2 hours, or until completely chilled.

8. **For the Topping:** Swirl the whipped cream on top of each cheesecake pie using a piping bag and 1M icing tip. Place one orange segment on top of each swirl.

Coconut Key Lime Cheesecake Pie

PREP TIME: 35 MINUTES | BAKE TIME: 45 MINUTES | SERVING: MAKES ONE 10-INCH PIE (12 SLICES)

I can't help it. I'm crazy for coconut, and hopefully you are, too. One of my husband's favorite pies is a key lime pie. So for this fun cheesecake, I added my beloved coconut to the cookie crust and filled it with a creamy key lime cheesecake. Oh my word! One bite of this tart cheesecake pie and you will be transported to a tropical place. Don't like coconut? Go ahead and use a regular cookie or cracker crust instead.

INGREDIENTS

For the Crust

20 Golden Oreo cookies

2 cups sweetened shredded coconut

½ cup (1 stick) unsalted butter, melted

For the Cheesecake

2 (8-ounce) packages cream cheese, at room temperature

½ cup sugar

½ cup sour cream

¼ cup key lime juice

2 tablespoons all-purpose flour

2 large eggs

For the Topping

1 cup Cool Whip, thawed

¼ cup Toasted Coconut (page 30)

Key lime slices

INSTRUCTIONS

1. Preheat the oven to 350°F.

2. **For the Crust:** Place the cookies, cream filling included, in a food processor. Pulse until the cookies become crumbs.

3. Mix together the cookie crumbs, shredded coconut, and melted butter. Press the mixture firmly into the bottom and sides of a 10-inch deep-dish pie plate. Bake for 10 minutes. Remove the pie plate from the oven and place it on a wire rack. Let the crust cool. Keep the oven on.

4. Place a large rimmed baking sheet on the very bottom rack of the oven and fill it halfway with water.

5. **For the Cheesecake:** Beat the cream cheese until creamy. Add the sugar and sour cream and beat until smooth.

6. Add the lime juice and flour and beat until creamy.

7. Add the eggs one at a time, beating well after each addition. Make sure the eggs are fully incorporated, but do not overbeat. Spoon the cheesecake batter into the cooled crust.

8. Cover the edges of the crust with aluminum foil to keep them from getting too brown while baking.

9. Place the pie plate on the oven rack right above the tray of water. Bake the cheesecake for 45 minutes.

10. Remove the pie plate from the oven and place it on a wire rack. Let the cheesecake cool for 1 hour, then refrigerate it for 2 to 3 hours, or until completely chilled.

11. **For the Topping:** Swirl Cool Whip around the edge of the pie using a piping bag and 1M icing tip. Top each swirl with toasted coconut and a key lime slice.

Breakfast Cheesecakes

×

CHEESECAKE FOR BREAKFAST? YES, PLEASE!

Does eating cheesecake for breakfast sound crazy? Or completely necessary and 100% okay? I think you know my answer to that question! I'm all for healthy eating most of the time, but special mornings call for a pastry or a Danish...all with cheesecake added in, of course. I like to think of it as satisfying my dairy requirement for the day. It makes me feel all healthy like that.

Lemon Blueberry Cheesecake Tarts

PREP TIME: 45 MINUTES | **BAKE TIME:** 18 TO 20 MINUTES | **SERVING:** MAKES 12 TARTS

Cheesecake is perfectly acceptable for breakfast when it looks like a pastry, right? These easy little tarts are topped with lemon cheesecake and fresh blueberries. That's a double dose of fruit right there, in my opinion. And since cream cheese is dairy, you could even say this fits in the dairy category of the food pyramid. Just don't consult a nutritionist, or my theory will be blown out of the water.

INGREDIENTS

2 frozen puff pastry sheets, thawed

For the Cheesecake

1 (8-ounce) package cream cheese, at room temperature

¼ cup granulated sugar

¼ cup lemon juice, fresh or concentrate

2 tablespoons all-purpose flour

1 cup fresh blueberries

For the Glaze

1 cup powdered sugar

2 tablespoons lemon juice, fresh or concentrate

INSTRUCTIONS

1. Preheat the oven to 400°F.

2. Spread the puff pastry out on a floured surface. Cut each sheet into 6 rectangles and place them on a large baking sheet.

3. Use a fork to poke holes all over the rectangles, leaving a ½-inch border around the edge.

4. **For the Cheesecake:** Beat the cream cheese until creamy. Add the granulated sugar and beat until smooth.

5. Add the lemon juice and flour and beat until creamy.

6. Spread the cheesecake evenly on the pastry rectangles, making sure not to go past the fork holes around the edge. Top each tart with fresh blueberries.

7. Bake for 18 to 20 minutes. Remove the pan and let the tarts cool on the pan for 15 minutes.

8. Remove the tarts and place them on a wire rack to cool for 30 minutes more, then refrigerate them for 1 hour, or until completely chilled.

9. **For the Glaze:** Whisk together the powdered sugar and lemon juice. Drizzle the glaze over the tops of the chilled tarts.

Triple Berry Cheesecake Crepes

PREP TIME: 30 MINUTES | SERVING: MAKES 12 CREPES

A few years ago our family went out for breakfast at a fun restaurant in Chicago. There were so many delicious choices, like crepes and stuffed French toast, on the breakfast menu. After we came home, I decided to try making crepes in my own kitchen. Adding a fun cheesecake and fruit filling gave these breakfast crepes a fancy dessert twist. My husband said they looked just like the fancy breakfast from that restaurant.

INGREDIENTS

For the Crepes

1¼ cups all-purpose flour

1 tablespoon granulated sugar

¼ teaspoon salt

3 large eggs

½ cup milk

¼ cup water

4 tablespoons (½ stick) unsalted butter, melted

½ teaspoon vanilla extract

For the Cheesecake Filling

1 (8-ounce) package cream cheese, at room temperature

½ cup granulated sugar

½ teaspoon vanilla extract

½ cup heavy cream

For Serving

1 batch Fruit Filling (page 26; use 2 cups fresh raspberries, blackberries, and blueberries)

1 cup fresh berries

Powdered sugar, for dusting (optional)

INSTRUCTIONS

1. **For the Crepes:** Place the flour, granulated sugar, salt, eggs, milk, water, butter, and vanilla in a blender. Pulse a few times until the mixture is completely mixed together. Refrigerate the batter for 1 hour.

2. Heat a small skillet over medium-low heat. Spray the skillet with nonstick cooking spray. Wipe out the excess spray with a paper towel. Spoon 2 tablespoons of the batter into the center of the pan. Pick up the pan and gently swirl the pan around until the batter stops moving. Cook for 1 to 2 minutes on the first side, then flip the crepe over and cook for 30 seconds more.

3. As you finish the crepes, place them on a plate, separating them with wax paper to keep them from sticking together. Repeat until you have used all the batter. Let the crepes cool.

4. **For the Cheesecake Filling:** Beat the cream cheese until creamy. Add the granulated sugar, vanilla, and cream and beat on high until light and fluffy.

5. **Assembly:** Place a spoonful of the cheesecake filling down the center of each crepe.

6. Top it with a spoonful of fruit filling and gently roll up the crepe .

7. Serve these with extra fruit filling and fresh berries on top. Sprinkle with powdered sugar, if desired.

Chocolate Cheesecake Muffins

PREP TIME: 25 MINUTES | **BAKE TIME:** 16 TO 18 MINUTES | **SERVING:** MAKES 20 MUFFINS

Okay, so technically these probably should be called cupcakes. I mean, they are chocolate, have a swirl of cheesecake in them, and are baked in a cupcake pan. But since I prefer to call it a muffin tin when I make breakfast treats, we are calling these muffins today. My daughter thinks that all muffins should include chocolate chips. She is so my daughter. She also thinks that all muffins should be warmed up in the microwave to get the chocolate chips all nice and gooey. She is one smart cookie…or should it be muffin? Either way, cheesecake-swirled chocolate muffins are the perfect treat for special breakfasts, or for a fun midweek snack. It's your call.

INGREDIENTS

For the Muffins

½ cup (1 stick) unsalted butter, at room temperature

⅔ cup packed brown sugar

1 large egg

2 teaspoons vanilla extract

⅔ cup sour cream

1 teaspoon ground cinnamon

2 teaspoons baking powder

1 teaspoon baking soda

1 teaspoon salt

½ cup unsweetened cocoa powder

2 cups all-purpose flour

⅔ cup milk

1 cup mini chocolate chips

INSTRUCTIONS

1. Preheat the oven to 400°F. Line a cupcake pan with paper liners. Line eight wells of a second cupcake pan with paper liners.

2. **For the Muffins:** Beat the butter and brown sugar until creamy. Add the egg, vanilla, and sour cream and beat until smooth.

3. Stir together the cinnamon, baking powder, baking soda, salt, cocoa powder, and flour in a bowl. Slowly add the dry mixture and the milk to the butter mixture, alternating between the two.

4. Stir in the mini chocolate chips by hand. Set the batter aside.

5. **For the Cheesecake:** Beat the cream cheese until creamy. Add the granulated sugar and beat until smooth.

6. Add the egg and beat until fully incorporated. Do not overbeat the batter.

(continued)

Chocolate Cheesecake Muffins (continued)

For the Cheesecake

1 (8-ounce) package cream cheese, at room temperature

¼ cup granulated sugar

1 large egg

For the Topping

¼ cup mini chocolate chips

7. Place one spoonful of the muffin batter in the bottom of each cupcake liner. Spoon the cheesecake filling evenly over the top of the batter in the liners. Top each liner with the rest of the muffin batter.

8. **For the Topping:** Sprinkle the tops of the muffins with the mini chocolate chips.

9. Bake the muffins for 16 to 18 minutes. Remove the pan from the oven and let the muffins cool in the pan for 5 minutes, then gently remove them from the pan and place them on a wire rack to cool completely.

Cinnamon Apple Cheesecake Coffee Cake

PREP TIME: 25 MINUTES | **BAKE TIME:** 35 TO 40 MINUTES | **SERVING:** 24 PIECES

Whoever first said that coffee cake was a perfectly acceptable breakfast is my new favorite friend. Soft cake, creamy cheesecake, homemade apple pie filling, and crumbs all layered together create the most magical breakfast cake. It practically melts in your mouth. I honestly could not stop eating bite after bite, so I had to send the rest to church for everyone else to indulge on. Sharing is caring in my book, especially when someone else eats all the calories for me. So make this amazing cake and invite a friend over for coffee and a chat. Then send the rest of the cake home with her, so you do not consume the entire thing. Believe me, it could happen.

INGREDIENTS

For the Coffee Cake

¾ cup (1½ sticks) cold unsalted butter

2½ cups all-purpose flour

¾ cup granulated sugar

¾ cup packed brown sugar

1 teaspoon ground cinnamon

½ teaspoon ground nutmeg

½ teaspoon salt

1 teaspoon baking soda

1 large egg

1 cup buttermilk

For the Cheesecake

1 (8-ounce) package cream cheese

¼ cup granulated sugar

1 large egg

1½ cups Apple Pie Filling (page 28)

INSTRUCTIONS

1. Preheat the oven to 350°F. Spray a 9 x 13-inch baking pan with nonstick baking spray.

2. **For the Coffee Cake:** Mix together the butter, flour, sugars, cinnamon, nutmeg, and salt with a fork until soft crumbs form. Set aside ¾ cup of the crumbs.

3. Add the baking soda, egg, and buttermilk to the remaining crumbs and beat until everything is incorporated.

4. Spread the batter in the prepared pan and set it aside.

5. **For the Cheesecake:** Beat the cream cheese until creamy. Add the granulated sugar and beat until smooth.

6. Add the egg and beat until fully incorporated. Do not overbeat the batter. Spread the cheesecake over the batter in the prepared pan.

(continued)

For the Glaze

½ cup powdered sugar

4 teaspoons milk

7. Spoon the pie filling randomly over the cheesecake batter. Sprinkle the reserved crumbs over everything.

8. Bake for 35 to 40 minutes. Remove the pan from the oven and place it on a wire rack. Let the cheesecake coffee cake cool for 1 hour, then refrigerate it for 1 to 2 hours.

9. For the Glaze: Whisk together the powdered sugar and milk. Drizzle the glaze over the top of the cake.

Optional: Use your favorite pie filling in place of the apple filling.

Cherry Lime Cheesecake Braid

PREP TIME: 20 MINUTES | **BAKE TIME:** 18 TO 20 MINUTES | **SERVING:** MAKES 1 LARGE BRAID (9 SLICES)

I am a big fan of adding cheesecake to refrigerated dough to make quick and easy breakfast treats. After making the Black Cherry Ricotta Cheesecakes on page 86, I had a little bit of cherry pie filling leftover, so I combined it with a tart lime cheesecake batter and a can of refrigerated crescent rolls. The lime glaze and zest give the pastry an extra punch of flavor that will get you going in the morning.

INGREDIENTS

For the Cheesecake

1 (8-ounce) package cream cheese, at room temperature

¼ cup granulated sugar

1 teaspoon lime juice, fresh or concentrate

For the Rolls

1 (8-count) tube refrigerated crescent rolls

½ cup Fruit Filling (page 26; use frozen cherries)

1 large egg

1 tablespoon water

1 teaspoon turbinado sugar

For the Glaze

2 cups powdered sugar

2 teaspoons lime juice, fresh or concentrate

Lime zest

INSTRUCTIONS

1. Preheat the oven to 375°F.

2. **For the Cheesecake:** Beat the cream cheese until creamy. Add the granulated sugar and lime juice and beat until smooth.

3. **For the Rolls:** Unroll the package of crescent rolls on a baking sheet and press together all the seams. Use a knife to cut strips along both sides of the dough, leaving 2 inches in the center uncut.

4. Spread the cheesecake mixture down the center of the dough. Top with the fruit filling.

5. Alternately place the dough strips across the filling, creating a braid pattern.

6. Whisk together the egg and water. Use a pastry brush to brush the egg mixture over the top of the braid. Sprinkle with the turbinado sugar.

7. Bake for 18 to 20 minutes. Remove the pan from the oven and let the braid cool for 1 hour, then refrigerate it for 1 hour until chilled.

8. **For the Glaze:** Whisk together the powdered sugar and lime juice. Drizzle over the braid and sprinkle with lime zest.

Banana Strawberry Cheesecake Sweet Rolls

PREP TIME: 1 HOUR | BAKE TIME: 20 MINUTES | SERVING: MAKES 12 ROLLS

Cinnamon rolls are one of my favorite things to make for weekend breakfast. I used to only make them from a can, from store-bought crescent rolls, or from a batter made without yeast. Why? Baking with yeast used to scare me. I thought there was no way I could make fluffy bread dough. One day I decided to get over my fear of that little packet and make my own dough. Imagine my surprise when making yeast dough turned out to actually be easier than I imagined. Trust me. You can do it, too! Just make sure you have enough time for the entire rising process. These soft fluffy banana rolls are filled with a creamy strawberry cheesecake. I'm all for adding more fruit and dairy to all the breakfast foods in my life!

INGREDIENTS

For the Dough

1 cup milk

4 tablespoons (½ stick) unsalted butter

3½ to 4 cups all-purpose flour

2 tablespoons granulated sugar

½ teaspoon salt

1 (¼ ounce) envelope rapid-rise yeast

½ cup mashed ripe banana

For the Cheesecake Filling

½ (8-ounce) package cream cheese, at room temperature

¾ cup strawberry pie filling

For the Frosting

2 ounces cream cheese, at room temperature

2 tablespoons milk

1 cup powdered sugar

INSTRUCTIONS

1. **For the Dough:** Place the milk and butter in a small saucepan over low heat. Stir it continuously until melted and warm to the touch. Remove the pan from the heat.

2. Stir together 3½ cups of the flour, the granulated sugar, and the salt in a bowl. Set aside.

3. Whisk the warm milk and yeast together. Pour the milk and mashed banana into the flour mixture and beat on low using a dough hook until a soft dough forms. If it is too sticky, add the remaining flour ¼ cup at a time until the dough pulls away from the bowl.

4. Gather the dough together into a ball and place it on a floured surface. Knead the dough ten times, or until it is smooth. Place the dough into a greased bowl, cover the top of the bowl with a damp towel, and let it rest for 10 to 15 minutes.

(continued)

5. Preheat the oven to 350°F. Butter a 9 x 13-inch baking dish.

6. For the Cheesecake Filling: Beat the cream cheese until creamy. Add the pie filling and beat again.

7. Roll the dough out on a floured surface into a 14 x 10-inch rectangle. Spread the cheesecake filling over the dough, leaving a 1-inch border all around the edges.

8. Beginning on one long edge, start to roll the dough up tightly. Pinch the seams together when you get to the end. Cut off the ends to even it up, and then cut the dough log crosswise into 12 even slices.

9. Place each slice in the prepared baking dish, cut-side down. Cover the top of the dish with a damp towel and place it in a warm place. Let the rolls rise for 20 minutes.

10. Remove the towel and place the pan in the oven. Bake the rolls for 20 minutes. Remove the pan from the oven and let the rolls cool slightly.

11. For the Frosting: Beat the cream cheese until creamy. Slowly add the milk and powdered sugar and beat again until smooth. Spread or drizzle the frosting over the tops of the warm rolls.

Cheesecake Nutella Pockets

PREP TIME: 30 MINUTES | **BAKE TIME:** 10 TO 11 MINUTES | **SERVING:** MAKES 8 POCKETS

I created these fun little pastry rolls one day as a special breakfast treat. Most days we do cereal, Pop-Tarts, or smoothies, but every once in a while cheesecake and chocolate make the morning go a little bit more smoothly. My kids love eating these as an after-school snack, too.

INGREDIENTS

For the Cheesecake

1 (8-ounce) package cream cheese, at room temperature

¼ cup sugar

1 large egg

For the Rolls

2 (8-ounce) tubes refrigerated crescent rolls

1 cup Nutella spread

For the Topping

1 ounce white baking chocolate

INSTRUCTIONS

1. Preheat the oven to 375°F.

2. **For the Cheesecake:** Beat the cream cheese until creamy. Add the sugar and beat until smooth.

3. Add the egg and beat until fully incorporated. Do not overbeat the batter

4. **For the Rolls:** Unroll the crescent rolls and separate the rolls into triangles. Press two triangles together to form a rectangle. Repeat until you have eight rectangles. Place the rectangles on a large baking sheet.

5. Spoon a large spoonful of Nutella and a large spoonful of cheesecake batter on one side of each rectangle.

6. Fold the other half of the dough over the filling. Press the seams together using a fork.

7. Bake for 10 to 11 minutes.

8. Remove the pan from the oven and let the pockets cool on the pan for a few minutes. Remove the pockets from the pan and place them on a wire rack to cool for 30 minutes, then transfer to the refrigerator to cool completely.

9. **For the Topping:** Melt the white chocolate according to the package directions. Stir until creamy. Drizzle over the cooled pockets.

Piña Colada Cheesecake Rolls

PREP TIME: 25 MINUTES | **BAKE TIME:** 10 TO 11 MINUTES | **SERVING:** MAKES 8 ROLLS

Coconut and pineapple are usually the two ingredients I reach for when I need a little bit of tropical flair in my life. These easy rolls are filled with a creamy coconut, pineapple, and cherry cheesecake filling. A drizzle of white chocolate and toasted coconut makes them look extra fancy. These would make great snacks for breakfast or for a bridal shower.

INGREDIENTS

For the Cheesecake

1 (8-ounce) package cream cheese, at room temperature

¼ cup sugar

½ teaspoon rum extract

¼ cup crushed pineapple, drained very well

¼ cup diced maraschino cherries, patted dry

½ cup sweetened shredded coconut

For the Rolls

2 (8-count) tubes refrigerated crescent rolls

For the Topping

⅓ cup white chocolate melts

¼ cup Toasted Coconut (page 30)

INSTRUCTIONS

1. Preheat the oven to 375°F.

2. **For the Cheesecake:** Beat the cream cheese until creamy. Add the sugar and rum extract and beat until smooth. Stir in the pineapple, cherries, and shredded coconut.

3. **For the Rolls:** Unroll the crescent rolls. Separate the rolls at the seams. Press two triangles together to form a rectangle. Repeat until you have eight rectangles. Place the rectangles on a large baking sheet.

4. Spoon the cheesecake filling down the centers of the rectangles. Fold the edges of the dough over the filling and press together the seams. Press together the ends of each roll as well. Flip the rolls over so the seam side is down.

5. Bake for 10 to 11 minutes. Remove the pan from the oven and let the rolls cool on the pan for 15 minutes. Remove them from the pan and refrigerate for 1 hour, or until chilled.

6. **For the Topping:** Melt the chocolate melts according to the package directions. Drizzle over the tops of the chilled rolls. Sprinkle with the toasted coconut.

Out-of-the-Box Cheesecake Desserts

×

FUN, FUN, FUN!

Still interested in adding cheesecake to more treats? Of course you are! Let me show you how easy it is to add cheesecake layers to cakes and to incorporate that cheesecake flavor into fudge, frosting, and cookies. I'll also share my recipe for Hot Chocolate Cheesecake Dip (page 205), which after just two weeks online, became one of my ten most popular recipes of 2014. Cheesecake to the extreme, here we come!

Pecan Cookie Dough Cheesecake Fudge

PREP TIME: 25 MINUTES | **SERVING:** MAKES 36 FUDGE SQUARES

Fudge is one of those treats that most people only make around the holidays. I have decided it is my goal in life to make fudge acceptable all year round, though. I love that this creamy white fudge is loaded with cookie dough bites and pecans. Adding the pecan bits incorporates that sweet-and-salty twist to this out-of-the-box wonder.

INGREDIENTS

1 (8-ounce) package cream cheese, at room temperature

2 cups white chocolate chips

4 cups powdered sugar

1 teaspoon vanilla extract

¾ cups plus 2 tablespoons finely chopped pecans

1 batch Cookie Dough Bites (page 23), frozen

INSTRUCTIONS

1. Line an 8-inch square baking pan with aluminum foil.

2. Beat the cream cheese until creamy.

3. Place the white chocolate chips in a microwave-safe bowl. Microwave for 30 seconds. Stir until melted and creamy. Heat for 15 seconds more, if needed.

4. Spoon the melted chocolate into the cream cheese and beat until smooth.

5. Add the vanilla and beat again. Slowly add the powdered sugar until it has been completely incorporated into the cream cheese mixture. The mixture will start to get thick.

6. Stir in ¾ cup of the chopped pecan and the frozen cookie dough bites gently with a stiff rubber spatula. Press the fudge mixture evenly into the prepared pan.

7. Sprinkle the remaining 2 tablespoons chopped pecan over the fudge and gently press them into the top. Let the fudge set for a few hours before lifting the foil out of the pan. Gently pull the foil off the fudge.

8. Run a sharp knife under hot water, then dry it off. Cut 36 fudge squares. Clean the knife often for clean cuts.

Note. Add mini chocolate chips, sprinkles, or mini M&M's in place of the nuts, if desired.

Cookies-and-Cream Cheesecake-Stuffed Strawberries

PREP TIME: 30 MINUTES | **SERVING:** MAKES 16 STRAWBERRIES

Our three kids are berry monsters who will eat an entire box if I'm not watching. I am so glad our kids love to eat fresh fruit and veggies. So when I bought a new big box of strawberries, I had to make sure everyone knew they had to wait to start munching. Many people like chocolate-covered strawberries, but I decided to try a different twist. These berries had a date with a cookies-and-cream cheesecake filling. These little treats would be so pretty on a shower or party table.

INGREDIENTS

½ (8-ounce) package cream cheese, at room temperature

2 tablespoons sugar

¼ cup heavy cream

2 Oreo cookies

16 fresh strawberries

16 mini Oreo cookies

INSTRUCTIONS

1. Beat the cream cheese and sugar until creamy. Add the cream and beat on high for 2 minutes.

2. Place the cookies, cream filling included, in a food processor. Pulse until the cookies become crumbs.

3. Gently stir the cookie crumbs into the cheesecake mixture.

4. Cut the leaves off the strawberries. Use a sharp paring knife to cut out the center of each strawberry. Cut a small slice off the bottom of each berry, so the strawberry will stand up straight when placed on a plate.

5. Fill each strawberry cavity with the cheesecake mixture using a piping bag and icing tip 27. Top each strawberry with a mini cookie immediately before serving.

Hot Chocolate Cheesecake Dip

PREP TIME: 15 MINUTES | **SERVING:** MAKES 2 CUPS

When the weather gets chilly and snowy, I like to snuggle up by the fire with a blanket and a cup of hot chocolate. I made this chocolate cheesecake dip a few years ago, and it has been extremely popular on the blog. The creamy cheesecake dip gets the chocolate flavor from powdered hot chocolate mix. Adding the fun topping makes it look like the bowl of dip is a big cup of hot cocoa! Try eating it with any kind of cookie, pretzel, or fruit! Of course, I went with the spoon option. What? You know that's how you want to eat it, too.

INGREDIENTS

1 (8-ounce) package cream cheese, at room temperature

½ cup plain Greek yogurt

½ cup marshmallow crème

1 cup instant dark hot cocoa mix

¾ cup Cool Whip

1 tablespoon mini marshmallow bits

Cookies and fruit, for serving

INSTRUCTIONS

1. Beat the cream cheese until creamy. Add the yogurt and marshmallow crème and beat until smooth.

2. Add the cocoa mix and beat until creamy.

3. Fold in ½ cup of the Cool Whip gently with a rubber spatula.

4. Spoon the cheesecake dip into a serving bowl. Top it with the remaining ¼ cup Cool Whip and the mini marshmallow bits.

5. Serve the dip with an assortment of cookies and fruit.

Cookies-and-Cream Cheesecake Cake Roll

PREP TIME: 40 MINUTES | **BAKE TIME:** 12 MINUTES | **SERVING:** MAKES ONE CAKE ROLL (10 SLICES)

Cake rolls used to scare me, until I figured out that they are actually quite easy to do. You just have to remember to roll them up while they are still hot; otherwise, you will end up with your cake in pieces. I like to place a piece of parchment paper on top of my roll instead of using powdered sugar to keep it from sticking. Our oldest son said the creamy cookies-and-cream filling made this cake roll taste like a giant Oreo cookie. I think he downed three slices in one day, or was it one hour? Oh, to have a teenager's metabolism again.

INGREDIENTS

For the Cake

3 large eggs

¾ cup granulated sugar

1 teaspoon vanilla extract

1 teaspoon baking powder

¾ cup all-purpose flour

¼ cup unsweetened dark cocoa powder

¼ teaspoon salt

½ cup milk

For the Cheesecake Filling

1 (8-ounce) package cream cheese

½ cup powdered sugar

1 cup Cool Whip, thawed

5 Oreo cookies

For the Topping

¼ cup heavy cream

¾ cup dark chocolate chips

5 Oreo cookies, chopped into chunks

INSTRUCTIONS

1. Preheat the oven to 375°F. Line a sturdy 15 x 10-inch rimmed baking sheet with foil-lined parchment paper, foil-side down. Spray the parchment paper with nonstick baking spray.

2. **For the Cake:** Beat the eggs for 3 to 5 minutes, until they are thick and dark yellow colored. Add the granulated sugar and vanilla and beat until incorporated.

3. Stir together the baking powder, flour, cocoa powder, and salt in a bowl. Add the flour mixture and milk alternately to the eggs and beat until everything is incorporated.

4. Spread the batter evenly in the prepared pan. Bake for 12 minutes.

5. Remove the pan from the oven and place it on a wire rack. Let cool for 2 to 3 minutes. Loosen the foil from the pan and lift it out. Flip the cake out of the pan onto a sheet of parchment paper. Pull off the original parchment paper slowly.

(continued)

6. Roll the cake up with the parchment paper immediately and place it on a wire rack. Do not unroll the cake until completely cool to the touch.

7. <u>**For the Cheesecake Filling:**</u> Beat the cream cheese until creamy. Add the powdered sugar and beat until smooth. Gently fold in the Cool Whip with a rubber spatula.

8. Place the cookies, cream filling included, in a food processor. Pulse until the cookies are crumbs. Stir the crumbs into the cheesecake mixture.

9. Unroll the cake, peeling off the parchment paper carefully. Spread the cheesecake filling evenly over the cake, leaving a 1-inch border all around. Roll the cake up tightly and refrigerate it for at least 1 hour.

10. <u>**For the Topping:**</u> Place the heavy cream and chocolate chips in a microwave-safe bowl. Microwave for 20 to 30 seconds. Stir the chocolate until melted and creamy.

11. Place the cake roll on a wire rack set over a baking sheet. Pour the melted chocolate down the center of the cake.

12. Use an offset spatula to spread the chocolate over the whole cake. As the chocolate rolls down the sides, use the spatula to spread it back onto the sides and top of the cake.

13. Once the chocolate has stopped moving, sprinkle the top of the chocolate with the cookie chunks. Let the chocolate set before cutting.

Chocolate Mint Cheesecake Ball

PREP TIME: 20 MINUTES | **SERVING:** MAKES 1 CHEESE BALL (SERVES 6 TO 8)

Chocolate, mint, and cheesecake, all in one glorious ball of goodness: it's bound to put smiles on everyone's faces as they use cookies and sweet crackers to scoop up bites of this creamy goodness. This fun cheese ball is great for parties and holidays. Such an easy treat with an explosion of flavor in every bite!

INGREDIENTS

1 (8-ounce) package cream cheese, at room temperature

½ cup (1 stick) unsalted butter, at room temperature

½ teaspoon vanilla extract

2 cups powdered sugar

¼ cup unsweetened cocoa powder

1¼ cups chocolate mint baking chips

Chocolate graham crackers, cookies, or pretzels, for serving

INSTRUCTIONS

1. Beat the cream cheese, butter, and vanilla until creamy.

2. Slowly add the powdered sugar and cocoa powder until everything has been incorporated. Beat on high for 1 minute.

3. Stir in ½ cup of the chocolate mint chips gently with a spoon.

4. Place a piece of plastic wrap inside a bowl. Spoon the cheesecake mixture into the bowl. Pull the plastic wrap up and shape the mixture into a ball. Twist the top of the plastic tight and place the cheese ball back into the bowl. Refrigerate the cheese ball for 1 to 2 hours or until firm.

5. Place the remaining chocolate mint chips on a plate. Unwrap the cheese ball and place it in the center of the mint chips. Roll the ball slowly until covered in the mint chips. You may need to use your hands to press the chips into some places. Serve the cheese ball with chocolate graham crackers, cookies, or pretzels.

Fruit Cheesecake Cookie Pizza

PREP TIME: 25 MINUTES   **BAKE TIME:** 15 MINUTES   **SERVING:** MAKES ONE 14-INCH PIZZA (14 SLICES)

We eat a lot of pizza in our house. My husband, his brothers, and my father-in-law opened their own pizza place in 2001. Although we didn't make a big living from this short-lived venture, they enjoyed creating unique pizza combinations. To this day, pizza is still one of our go-to meals on the weekends. If you like unique pizza combos, you need to try adding cheesecake filling and fresh fruit to the top of a giant cookie pizza. And yes, this is a pizza, despite what my husband thinks. After all, it has a crust, cheese, and toppings…all the makings of a pizza! I think he just rolled his eyes at me.

INGREDIENTS

1 batch Cookie Dough (page 31)

For the Cheesecake Topping

1 (8-ounce) package cream cheese, at room temperature

½ cup granulated sugar

1 teaspoon vanilla extract

1 cup Cool Whip, thawed

For the Fruit Topping

1 (15-ounce) can mandarin oranges, drained

1 fresh kiwi, peeled and sliced

1 cup sliced strawberries

1 pint blueberries

½ pint blackberries

½ pint raspberries

INSTRUCTIONS

1. Preheat the oven to 375°F. Spray a 14-inch pizza pan with nonstick spray.

2. Press the cookie dough into an even 12-inch circle on the prepared pan.

3. Bake for 15 minutes. Remove the pan from the oven and let the cookie crust cool completely.

4. **For the Cheesecake Topping:** Beat the cream cheese until creamy. Add the granulated sugar and vanilla and beat until smooth.

5. Gently fold in the Cool Whip using a rubber spatula. Spread the cheesecake filling evenly over the cooled cookie.

6. **For the Fruit Topping:** Arrange the fruit in a fun pattern on top of the cheesecake filling.

Rocky Road Cheesecake Cake

PREP TIME: 1 HOUR | BAKE TIME: 65 MINUTES | SERVING: MAKES ONE 8-INCH LAYER CAKE (14 SLICES)

Even though ice cream is not my favorite dessert, I do enjoy a bowl of rocky road ice cream from time to time. Soft marshmallow mixed with chocolate and nuts—swoon! I decided to add all those flavors to one incredible layer cake. Trust me, this cheesecake cake will knock your socks off. The recipe does take some time to prepare, but after one slice of cake, you will be so happy that you took the time to make it.

INGREDIENTS

For the Cheesecake

2 (8-ounce) packages cream cheese, at room temperature

½ cup granulated sugar

½ cup sour cream

1 teaspoon vanilla extract

1 cup marshmallow crème

2 large eggs

For the Cake

1 (15.25-ounce) box chocolate cake mix

3 large eggs

½ cup canola oil

½ cup sour cream

1 cup milk

2 tablespoons unsweetened cocoa powder

(continued)

INSTRUCTIONS

1. Place a large rimmed baking sheet on the bottom rack of the oven and fill it halfway with water. Preheat the oven to 350°F. Line an 8-inch springform pan with parchment paper.

2. For the Cheesecake: Beat the cream cheese until creamy. Add the sugar, sour cream, and vanilla and beat until smooth. Add the marshmallow crème and beat again.

3. Add the eggs one a time, beating well after each addition. Make sure the eggs are fully incorporated, but do not overbeat the batter.

4. Pour the batter into the prepared springform pan. Place the pan on the oven rack right above the tray of water. Bake the cheesecake for 35 minutes.

5. Remove the pan from the oven and place it on a wire rack. Let cool for 5 minutes, and then run a sharp knife around the edge of the cheesecake to loosen it from the pan. Let the cheesecake cool for 1 hour, then refrigerate it for 4 to 6 hours, or until chilled.

6. Remove the pan of water from the oven. Preheat the oven to 350°F. Grease two 8-inch cake pans and dust them with cocoa powder, tapping out any excess.

(continued)

For the Frosting

½ cup (1 stick) unsalted butter, at room temperature

½ cup marshmallow crème

1/4 teaspoon salt

1 teaspoon vanilla extract

4 cups powdered sugar

6 tablespoons heavy cream

⅔ cup finely chopped pecans

For the Topping

¼ cup heavy cream

½ cup milk chocolate chips

2 tablespoons finely chopped pecans

2 tablespoons mini marshmallow bits

2 tablespoons mini chocolate chips

8 pecan halves

7. **For the Cake:** Combine the cake mix, eggs, oil, sour cream, and milk in a large bowl. Beat on low speed for 1 minute, then increase the speed to medium and beat for 2 minutes more.

8. Divide the batter between the prepared cake pans. Bake the cakes for 28 to 30 minutes, or until a toothpick inserted into the center comes out mostly clean.

9. Remove the pans from the oven and let the cakes cool in the pans for 15 minutes, then flip them out onto a wire rack. Let cool completely before frosting.

10. **For the Frosting:** Beat the butter until creamy. Add the marshmallow crème, salt, and vanilla and beat until smooth.

11. Add the powdered sugar and cream alternately to the butter mixture until everything has been incorporated. Beat on high for a few minutes, until light and fluffy.

12. If needed, cut off the tops of the cakes to make them level. Place one cake layer on a serving plate. Place the chilled cheesecake on top of the cake. Top with the remaining cake layer. Use a sharp knife to even the sides of the cake and the cheesecake so they are flush.

13. Set aside ¼ cup of the frosting. Use an offset spatula to cover the entire cake evenly with the frosting. Smooth the frosting out with the edge of the spatula. Let the frosting sit for 20 minutes, and then use a piece of parchment paper to smooth the frosting out.

14. Press the pecan chips around the bottom half of the cake by cupping your hands and pressing the chips into the frosting slowly.

15. <u>For the Topping:</u> Place the heavy cream and chocolate chips in a microwave-safe bowl. Microwave for 20 to 30 seconds. Stir the chocolate until melted and creamy. Let cool slightly. Spoon the chocolate onto the top of the cake. Use an offset spatula to spread the chocolate around the top without going over the edges.

16. Sprinkle the chocolate with the pecan bits, marshmallow bits, and mini chocolate chips before it sets. Transfer the reserved frosting to a piping bag fitted with frosting tip 27 and pipe the frosting in swirls around the top of the cake. Top each swirl with a pecan half.

Vanilla Funfetti Cheesecake Dip

PREP TIME: 10 MINUTES | **SERVING:** MAKES 2 CUPS

Sprinkles and vanilla bean flecks add a delicious flavor and pretty effect to this easy dip. This sweet dip is perfect for serving at parties as a dessert appetizer. We love using chocolate chip cookies, pretzels, and strawberries to eat this dip. Just restrain yourself from diving headfirst into the bowl…at least in front of people.

INGREDIENTS

1 (8-ounce) package cream cheese, at room temperature

1 cup powdered sugar

1 tablespoon vanilla bean paste

½ cup heavy cream

¼ cup rainbow jimmies

Fruit and cookies, for serving

INSTRUCTIONS

1. Beat the cream cheese until creamy. Add the powdered sugar and vanilla bean paste and beat until smooth.

2. Add the cream and beat on low until creamy. Increase the speed to high and beat for 2 to 4 minutes, or until light and fluffy.

3. Gently stir in the sprinkles. Refrigerate the mixture for 1 to 2 hours, or until it sets up. Serve with fruit and cookies.

M&M's Cookie Cups with Nutella Cheesecake Frosting

PREP TIME: 35 MINUTES | **BAKE TIME:** 12 MINUTES | **SERVING:** MAKES 24 COOKIES

These little cookie cups are bursting with color and flavor. The soft cookie base is loaded with mini M&M's candies, but what really sets these cookies apart is the creamy cheesecake topping. Nutella lovers will fall in love with the creamy frosting swirls. A sprinkling of more candies on top makes these cookies a fun treat for any party.

INGREDIENTS

For the Cookies

1½ cups mini M&M's candies

1 batch Cookie Dough (page 31)

For the Frosting

1 (8-ounce) package cream cheese, at room temperature

1 cup Nutella spread

1 teaspoon vanilla extract

½ teaspoon salt

4 cups powdered sugar

6 tablespoons heavy cream

INSTRUCTIONS

1. Preheat the oven to 375°F. Spray two 12-cavity mini-tart pans with nonstick baking spray.

2. <u>For the Cookies:</u> Gently stir 1 cup of the mini M&M's candies into the cookie dough.

3. Roll the dough into 24 even balls. Place one dough ball in each cavity of the prepared pans. Bake for 12 minutes.

4. Remove the pans from the oven and let the cookies cool in the pans for 2 minutes, before pressing in the centers with a tart shaper. Gently remove the cookies from the pans and place them on a wire rack to cool completely before frosting.

5. <u>For the Frosting:</u> Beat the cream cheese until creamy. Add the Nutella, vanilla, and salt and beat until smooth.

6. Add the powdered sugar and cream alternately until everything has been completely incorporated. Beat on high for 1 to 2 minutes, or until light and fluffy.

(continued)

7. Transfer the frosting to a piping bag fitted with frosting tip 1M. Pipe the frosting into the cooled cookie cups. Sprinkle the remaining M&M's on the top of the frosting.

Note

» Change out the M&M's candies for other candy bars or chocolates. Use crushed-up Butterfinger bars, chopped peanut butter cups, or mini chocolate chips.

» Add another 2 tablespoons heavy cream to the frosting and use it to frost your favorite cupcakes.

Mini Hot Chocolate Cheesecake Tarts

PREP TIME: 20 MINUTES | BAKE TIME: 22 MINUTES | SERVING: MAKES 12 MINI TARTS

I think that all cups of hot chocolate should be topped with Cool Whip and sprinkles. A steamy mug of chocolate seems so much more fun and delicious when it is given a sprinkle of rainbow colors! These little tarts have a chocolate cookie crust, a creamy hot chocolate cheesecake, and a swirl of Cool Whip with sprinkles for fun. They are such an easy treat to make and taste incredible.

INGREDIENTS

For the Crust

1½ cups chocolate graham cracker crumbs

2 tablespoons sugar

½ cup (1 stick) unsalted butter, melted

For the Cheesecake

1 (8-ounce) package cream cheese, at room temperature

2 tablespoons sugar

½ teaspoon vanilla extract

½ cup dry hot chocolate mix

1 large egg

For the Topping

1 cup Cool Whip, thawed

½ cup mini marshmallow bits

2 tablespoons rainbow jimmies

INSTRUCTIONS

1. Preheat the oven to 350°F.

2. **For the Crust:** Mix together the graham cracker crumbs, sugar, and melted butter. Spoon the mixture evenly into a 12-cavity mini-tart pan. Press the crumbs firmly into the bottom and up the sides of each well. Set the pan on a rimmed baking sheet.

3. Bake the tart shells for 8 minutes. Remove from the oven and let the crusts cool in the pan.

4. **For the Cheesecake:** Beat the cream cheese until creamy. Add the sugar and vanilla and beat until smooth. Add the hot chocolate mix and beat until incorporated.

5. Add the egg and beat until fully incorporated. Do not overbeat the batter. Divide the batter evenly among the prepared tart shells.

6. Bake for 22 minutes. Remove from the oven and let the cheesecakes cool in the pan for 15 minutes. Gently remove each cheesecake from the pan and let them cool for 1 hour on a wire rack.

7. Refrigerate the cheesecakes for 1 to 2 hours or until completely chilled.

8. **For the Topping:** Top with Cool Whip using a piping bag and icing tip 1M. Sprinkle the swirls with mini marshmallows and sprinkles.

Piña Colada Cheesecake Cake Trifle

PREP TIME: 1 HOUR | **BAKE TIME:** 30 MINUTES | **SERVING:** MAKES ONE LARGE TRIFLE (14 SERVINGS)

One of my favorite things to do at the beach, other than sleep in the sun, is to build sand castles. I am not a big fan of being in the ocean—thank you, *Jaws*, for ruining that for me when I was younger. But hand me a bucket and a shovel, and I will be happy to build you something. Building a cake trifle is sort of like building a sand castle. There is a large bowl, layers of cake, a creamy no-bake coconut cheesecake, and fruit to work with. This summer dessert will definitely have you thinking of the beach after one bite!

INGREDIENTS

For the Cake

1 (20-ounce) can crushed pineapple

1 (15¼ ounce) vanilla cake mix

For the Cheesecake

1 (8-ounce) package cream cheese, at room temperature

1 (3.4-ounce) box instant vanilla pudding

1 cup milk

1 cup sweetened shredded coconut

½ teaspoon rum extract

½ teaspoon coconut extract

2½ cups Cool Whip, thawed

1 (16-ounce) jar maraschino cherries with stems

¼ cup Toasted Coconut (page 30)

INSTRUCTIONS

1. Preheat the oven to 350°F. Spray a 9 x 13-inch baking pan with nonstick baking spray.

2. **For the Cake:** Drain the crushed pineapple, saving the juice.

3. Prepare the cake mix, using the pineapple juice in place of the liquid called for on the box.

4. Spread the cake batter in the prepared pan. Bake according to the directions on the box.

5. Remove the pan from the oven and let the cake cool completely. Cut the cooled cake into 1-inch cubes.

6. **For the Cheesecake:** Beat the cream cheese until creamy. Set aside.

7. Whisk the dry pudding mix into the milk until it thickens.

8. Slowly add the thickened pudding and extracts to the cream cheese. Beat on low until the mixture is smooth and creamy.

9. Stir in the shredded coconut, then gently fold in 1 cup of the Cool Whip with a rubber spatula.

10. Drain the cherries and set aside 10 of them, with stems, for the top. Remove the stems from the remaining cherries and cut them in half. Pat them dry with a paper towel.

11. Place 4 cups of the cake cubes in the bottom of a large trifle bowl. Spoon half the drained pineapple on top of the cake, followed by half the cherries.

12. Gently spread half the cheesecake pudding mixture on top of the fruit. Repeat the layers again, ending with the cheesecake pudding.

13. Sprinkle the top of the cheesecake with the toasted coconut. Swirl the remaining 1½ cups Cool Whip around the edges and in the middle of the trifle with a piping bag fitted with icing tip 1M. Place the reserved cherries on the swirls.

Acknowledgments

I still cannot believe that I am sitting here writing thank-yous for my very own cookbook. If someone would have told me four years ago that I would be running a successful baking blog and writing a book all about my favorite dessert, I probably would have laughed out loud. It blows my mind to think of how far my blogging hobby has come. All praise goes to God for guiding me and leading me through this fun journey. God has given me a job that I absolutely love and enjoy, and I am so thankful for His blessings and provisions.

First of all, I want to thank my husband, Jeremy. You are my biggest supporter and champion in everything I do. It's because of you that I am who I am today. I appreciate your support and encouragement so much. Thank you so much for believing in me from day one, helping me test recipes, and reading and proofing my drafts. Thank you for running to the store at all hours for missing ingredients, for talking me down from the ledge a few times, and for reminding me that I could do this. You are my rock. I love you so much, and I'm so thankful that God placed you in my life.

A special thank-you goes out to my three children, Cameron, Cassie, and Caedon, for putting up with some craziness for a few months as I made dozens and dozens of desserts instead of dinner. Thank you for doing your chores, helping out with cleaning, and for not complaining when we had cereal or quesadillas for dinner, again. You made it easy to keep pressing on.

Thank you to my family and to my parents for being my number one fans through the years. I appreciate how you continue to support me by reading, liking, and sharing my recipes on Facebook.

I am so thankful for all my old and new friends from near and far who encouraged and prayed for me as I worked on this book. Your support and prayers helped me stay strong.

I want to thank all of my faithful blog readers from over the years. Without you and your sweet comments, I would not have continued sharing our life through recipes for this many years. Thank you for reading, commenting, and making the blog a success. It's because of your love for my recipes that I decided to write this cookbook. Thank you for making the recipes for your family and friends. It means so much to me.

Thank you to my agent, Maria, at Stonesong for reaching out to me two years ago. Without all your help and guidance, I would not have had this amazing opportunity or come so far.

Thank you so much to the team at St. Martin's Press for all the hard work that went into editing and putting this book together. Thank you for having the patience and faith in my writing and photography skills.

A huge thank-you goes to Meagan from azestybite.com for stepping in last minute to help me with the photo edits. I still can't believe how fast you were able to have them done. Thank you for saving me so much time sitting at my computer. You made my photos look amazing!

Thank you so much to everyone at church who tasted recipes for me. I am so appreciative of your feedback and excitement as I brought boxes and boxes of cheesecake to church each week. Thank you for eating every last one, so I didn't have to take them home and eat more myself.

I want to thank all my blogging friends who encouraged me along the way. Thank you for being willing to listen and to answer all my questions about blogging and baking. I am so thankful to have met so many of you face to face at different blog events over the years. Blogging wouldn't be the same without your friendship, support, and community.

A special thank-you goes out to Aimee, Dorothy, and Ashton. You three were my very first blog friends, and I'm so thankful for your love and support over the years.

And finally, a huge thank-you to all of you for buying this book. I hope you enjoy getting in the kitchen and have some fun adding cheesecake to all the things.

Index